brilliant

verbal
reasoning

brilliant

verbal
reasoning

Robert Williams

Prentice Hall
is an imprint of

Harlow, England • London • New York • Boston • San Francisco • Toronto • Sydney • Singapore • Hong Kong
Tokyo • Seoul • Taipei • New Delhi • Cape Town • Madrid • Mexico City • Amsterdam • Munich • Paris • Milan

PEARSON EDUCATION LIMITED

Edinburgh Gate
Harlow CM20 2JE
Tel: +44 (0)1279 623623
Fax: +44 (0)1279 431059
Website: www.pearsoned.co.uk

First published in Great Britain in 2009

© Pearson Education Limited 2010

ISBN: 978-0-273-72453-7

British Library Cataloguing-in-Publication Data
A catalogue record for this book is available from the British Library

Library of Congress Cataloging-in-Publication Data
A catalog record for this book is available from the Library of Congress

10 9 8 7 6 5 4 3 2 1
14 13 12 11 10

Typeset in 10/14pt Plantin by 3
Printed in Great Britain by Henry Ling Ltd., at the Dorset Press, Dorchester, Dorset

The publisher's policy is to use paper manufactured from sustainable forests.

For Anne Marie – without whom this wouldn't have happened.

Contents

About the author

Rob Williams is a chartered occupational psychologist with over 12 years' experience in the design and delivery of ability tests. Having worked for several of the UK's leading test publishers, he has written many verbal reasoning tests and presented his research at home and abroad. Today he heads up Rob Williams Assessment Ltd, an independent company specialising in assessment for recruitment. Rob has run hundreds of assessment centres for numerous public sector organisations and private companies – giving him valuable insight into how testing is used in a wide range of businesses. When he's not working, Rob enjoys spending time with his two young daughters, going to the cinema and playing tennis.

To find out more see www.robwilliamsassessment.co.uk

Acknowledgements

I would like to thank the following people for their help with this book's practice questions: Helene Ryan, Stephanie Pliakas and my parents, Marion and Richard Williams.

While every effort has been taken to ensure that the practice questions in this book accurately replicate the actual tests, test formats do change periodically. It is therefore wise to always consult your testing organization's website for the most up-to-date information about your test.

Foreword

S trange things, multiple choice tests. I remember sitting school exams and having a sense of relief at one being 'only' a multiple choice test as if it was somehow a lot easier than having to construct something from scratch or have to actually think about an answer.

Well, that may be true. But there is a resultant false sense of security here that usually means one does less preparation for it because we know we can just guess if we don't know the answer. I don't recommend this as a strategy, however. At least, it never did me any good. Guessing is strictly overrated and if you are in competition with others (and who isn't these days?) then you will always be up against people who don't have to.

Luckily, when it comes to that all-important verbal reasoning test, there is another option. Read this book. Oh, and practise. There is a good reason for this. While our true verbal reasoning ability essentially remains fairly stable (unless we are actively working on it) we can make a large difference in our test results in being more test-aware – having a set of strategies in place to make sure we perform as well as we are able. This does not mean that the test itself is unreliable – far from it, in fact. It just means that having those strategies results in your score being more likely to reflect your true ability. All the 'process' mistakes have been ironed out and what is left is the 'content' – your real verbal reasoning ability. It is an unfortunate truth that no matter how good the test itself is, your score is not going to reflect how good you actually are unless you know how to perform at your best from a standing start, as it were. And this is where this book comes in.

Understanding how to both analyse and interpret written information is key to the vast majority of graduate (and increasingly, non-graduate) jobs out there. We build these skills slowly through our education, our interactions with those around us and also our reading, but like most things, if we don't make a conscious effort to grow our skills they tend to remain stubbornly and unreasonably static – or worse, actually reduce. This is why this book is needed. We don't fulfil our true potential in assessments because of factors that have little to do with our true ability – lack of familiarity with testing under time pressure and nervousness being just two.

In my 15 years as an occupational psychologist I have tested many hundreds of individuals and talked to many of them about their strategies for completing the test at a feedback session. The answer was usually quite simple: there wasn't one. Well, not if you don't include 'guessing and hoping to be a statistical anomaly'. Having a clear strategy in your head before you sit down is your best chance of performing well on the day. And practice, practice, practice, of course.

You never know – that may just stack the odds in your favour. And if that hasn't persuaded you, perhaps this will: tests of reasoning ability are among the most valid forms of occupational assessment there are. In other words, good scores on the test predict good job performance in the future better than most types of assessment. Which, of course, is why they are used.

And which is why you need this book.

Peter Storr, C. Psychol.
London
2009

Getting to grips with your test

You've probably bought this book because you are facing a verbal reasoning test. Perhaps you are worried that your verbal reasoning skills are not up to scratch. Maybe you are feeling nervous because it has been a long time since you've sat a formal test. Or it might be that you just want to get ahead of the competition by being better prepared. All of these are great reasons – they mean you are motivated to practise. Whether you are a beginner or an experienced test-taker you can benefit from more practice. The fact is that practice works: it is known to improve scores. This book, and a willingness to practise, can certainly help you improve your performance on test day. Let's look at how.

Try approaching your upcoming verbal reasoning test like a running race. You wouldn't just turn up at the starting line and hope for the best, would you? Instead, you'd go out for training runs in the preceding weeks – starting with easy jogs then building up to faster sprints. On the race day you'd want to be rested, relaxed, and in peak physical and mental condition. This book coaches you to prepare for your test in a similar way – by providing ample practice opportunities and strategies to use on your test day. You aren't striving for a gold medal here, but success in a verbal reasoning test may be a stepping stone to a new job, a promotion or a place on a degree course.

Test-taking technique is also crucial. Remember at school when your teacher would go over the format for your exams and review what was likely to come up? The same applies when facing an ability test – you need to know what to expect. As a psychometrician I have written many different types of verbal reasoning test. This has given me insights into the strange world of test design, so throughout this first section you'll find brilliant test-taking tips and tactics that really work. In short, here are all the tools you need to maximise your verbal reasoning performance.

CHAPTER 1

Getting
started

You know that you will soon be taking a verbal reasoning test, but you may be wondering what, exactly, is a verbal reasoning test? A verbal reasoning test is a type of ability test, some-

> A verbal reasoning test is a type of ability test

times referred to as a psychometric or aptitude test. It is designed to measure specific verbal abilities relevant for success in a particular course, profession or job. Verbal reasoning tests are an objective and accurate means of assessing a candidate's potential effectiveness whenever there is a verbal component to a particular job role or course.

When do I use verbal reasoning?

Your verbal reasoning skills may be something that you've taken for granted. Or you may have assumed that they are only relevant for people who like doing crosswords and playing Scrabble. In fact, reading comprehension is something that we all do every day in both our personal lives and at work. From newspapers and magazines to correspondence and company reports, you use your verbal reasoning skills to make sense of all different types of writing. Whether you are aware of it or not, you use your verbal reasoning skills when following a new recipe, reading a notice at a train station, applying for a bank account, or browsing through holiday brochures.

Who needs good verbal reasoning skills?

As you've seen above, *everyone* needs to have basic verbal reasoning skills to survive daily life. And *good* verbal reasoning skills are a key prerequisite for many different jobs. Any job that involves frequent communication requires verbal reasoning skills. This could mean written communication in emails or reports, or spoken and written communication such as in teaching. In a commercial environment, for instance, call centre employees need to be able to converse clearly with their customers. At the graduate and managerial levels, many jobs require the interpretation and critical analysis of complex verbal information.

> *good* verbal reasoning skills are a key prerequisite for many jobs

Almost all jobs require some form of verbal communication and/or reading written information. Internal correspondence with your colleagues can be more informal (depending upon who they are!) than when you are communicating with your customers or clients.

Let's have a look at a typical office environment and how different workers use verbal reasoning skills to perform their duties.

Graduate trainee

Recent graduates who have just started working on a training scheme will apply their verbal reasoning skills whenever they interact or correspond with other members of staff. They need to match their verbal communication to different levels of seniority and adjust their communication style to suit the formality of the meeting or event. Graduates may also need to prepare business reports. These should not read like an essay!

Managers/directors

Most managers will need to use higher levels of verbal reasoning when reading or preparing reports. They need to be able to adapt their spoken and written communication style to the situation, whether addressing their subordinates or customers/clients. Other company reporting procedures, such as appraisals, also require clearly written documentation.

Senior managers and directors will need to use the highest levels of verbal reasoning skills when analysing company reports, dealing with compliance issues and statutory obligations. Here there is a need for concise and accurate communication.

Customer service/sales roles

Effective oral communication is the key to handling customer queries or sales calls. Talking to customers on the phone or face to face demands a flexible communication style. For example, telesales personnel would be expected to respond differently to a customer who was complaining than to one who was a prospective sale. Persuasive presentation skills also rely upon a solid foundation of verbal reasoning skills.

PA or administrative roles

A PA's responsibilities typically include written correspondence, such as letters and emails, which need to use an appropriate tone and level for the intended audience. Administrative roles also need to check written documents, to file these accurately and to keep on top of plans and procedures that have been agreed orally or in writing.

Why do I need to take a test?

Verbal reasoning ability links to job performance, which is why verbal reasoning tests are now used as part of the selection criteria for certain professions and postgraduate degree courses in which it is essential to work effectively with verbal information. Many medium-sized and large employers also make extensive use of ability tests – such as verbal reasoning tests – as part of their standard recruitment and promotion processes. The overall aim is for the best people to be selected – and the use of ability tests differentiates the high performers from the low performers. A well-designed verbal reasoning test is a reliable and consistent means of assessing the skills required for effective performance in that working environment.

> the use of ability tests differentiates the high performers from the low performers

Ability tests allow employers and university admissions offices to assess a large number of applicants for competitive positions in a standardised way. The same ability test can be given to a large number of applicants and the results used as an efficient means of comparision. This standardisation makes the process much fairer than relying upon old-fashioned, unstructured interviews where every applicant would be asked different questions. Even if you don't like the idea of being tested on your verbal reasoning skills, at least you know that it is fair since everyone has to do the same test!

! brilliant warning

It is worth pointing out that the placing of people in jobs should not be carried out in a way that is solely dependent on their verbal reasoning test results.

How are verbal reasoning skills assessed?

There are many, many different types of verbal reasoning test at a variety of levels. These range from a basic test of your understanding of words to a detailed assessment of your comprehension of the different parts of an argued case. Verbal reasoning tests are continually updated and revised. Some question formats, such as those asking you to identify synonyms and antonyms, are less commonly used now. Although some tests of general intelligence may still use such questions, it has become very common to rely upon the passage of text format.

This book covers all the most common types of verbal reasoning question format. In Part 2 you will find chapters covering the following types of tests:

- Armed Forces entry tests (Chapter 7). These are basic literacy tests – testing your understanding of the meaning of words.

- Qualified Teacher Status (Chapter 8). The QTS Literacy Test assesses spelling, grammar, punctuation and reading comprehension.

- UKCAT (Chapter 9). This test format features passage-based questions, where you read a short text and answer associated questions.

- Graduate and managerial level tests (Chapter 10). These are advanced passage-based questions, which are often on business themes.

brilliant tip

Popular tests share similar formats, so if you want to further improve your verbal reasoning skills you can get extra practice by completing questions in other chapters that have a similar format to your test.

How can I prepare?

There's a lot you can do to prepare. I'll say it many, many times throughout the course of this book: the best way to improve your performance is through practice. This book features practice questions specially devised for every commonly used test format, allowing you to select the ones that you need most. You'll get the most benefit if you practise with questions that mirror the exact test you are preparing to take.

practise with questions that mirror the exact test you are preparing to take

There are many skills that you can practise in advance. The test-taker needs to concentrate, pay attention to detail and interpret the meaning of individual words and phrases as well as analysing the overall meaning of a text passage. When answering individual questions the test-taker needs to focus on extracting the relevant verbal information. Imagine yourself as an eagle, circling over the overall passage and then swooping down to zero in on your prey – i.e. the bit of information needed to answer the question correctly. The practice questions will help you hone these skills. I've also included suggestions for turning everyday activities into practice opportunities.

brilliant tip

Verbal reasoning tests are not as black and white as other ability tests. You may even be asked to respond 'Can't say' or 'Cannot tell' to certain questions.

How important is this test?

Broadly speaking, the earlier in an assessment process that you are being asked to complete a verbal reasoning test the more important it is to pass. Candidates who do not pass are sifted out of the process, allowing employers to focus on applicants whose skills are most suitable for the job.

You may be taking a verbal reasoning test as part of an assessment centre procedure where many different types of exercise – such as interviews, group exercises, presentations, role plays and other psychometric tests – are combined. Here the test is a part of several assessments and you will not be sifted out on the basis of the verbal reasoning test alone. That said, it is still important to pass – you don't want a poor performance in the test to let you down.

brilliant warning

Most of the test questions will be multiple choice. Don't be fooled into thinking that this makes them easier. The answer options are deliberately designed to catch out those who make sloppy errors.

brilliant recap

- Everyone uses verbal reasoning skills in both written and spoken communication.

- Verbal reasoning tests are a fair and objective way to assess large numbers of candidates. They are used because they predict future performance at work.

- There are many different types of verbal reasoning test on the market, at varying levels of difficulty.

- The best way to prepare for a verbal reasoning test is to practise with questions that mirror your actual test format.

CHAPTER 2

Practice makes perfect

Right, let's get down to work. First think about how much time you can spare for practising. Then set aside the time so you can conduct as many reading and practice sessions as possible over a period of several weeks or months. This is preferable to reading through this book in two or three sittings. You may like to set aside a particular time at the weekend, or a time of day when your mind is most alert. Once you've committed to a practice session, make sure you stick to it. Go on – start practising as soon as you can!

> start practising as soon as you can!

Why should I practise?

Does a virtuoso violinist ever quit practising? Of course not, she keeps practising so as to stay at the top of her game. There's a lot of truth to the old adage 'Practice makes perfect'. You're not striving for perfection here, but practising questions is known to significantly improve your chances of passing a verbal reasoning test. Try to squeeze in as much advance practice as possible. Make a commitment to practise as much as you can to improve your confidence and help you keep a clear head on the day. Continually review what you have learnt from previous practice test sessions so that you use your time most effectively.

How much practice do I need?

That depends on why you are taking the test and your current skill level. Your verbal reasoning test may be a key to a new stage in your life, such as joining the Armed Forces or studying for a medical degree. You may be seeking promotion or going for a great new job. Let's face it – whatever the scenario, you want to pass that test! Even if the outcome is not solely dependent on your verbal reasoning test score it is worth maximising your practice opportunities when entry to a future profession is at stake.

The time required to improve your verbal reasoning testing performance will vary between a few hours for those who are just a little bit rusty to several days for less experienced readers. Although they will need to put in more work, those who have not taken a verbal reasoning test before may well see the most dramatic improvement through practice.

brilliant tip

If you don't already know exactly what type of verbal reasoning test you will be taking, you should find out as your first step. That way you will know what type of questions you need to practise.

break down each practice session into three linked stages

Practice strategy

I suggest breaking down each practice session into three linked stages:

1 *before* taking a practice test

2 *during* the practice test

3 *after* taking a practice test

Before taking a practice test

- Plan which questions you are going to answer. Then you can get going straight away instead of wasting time flicking through the book.

- Identify a quiet place to work where you are unlikely to be disturbed. It is important to find an environment where you can read quietly and really concentrate.

- Set aside at least 40 minutes to work your way through a large number of the practice questions.

- Sit at a desk and clear away anything that may distract you before starting.

- Turn your mobile phone off.

- Have a clock or watch handy to time how quickly you work.

During the practice test

- Treat it as a real test session to help you get into the right mindset. This will help reduce any nerves on the test day, even if that day will certainly be more stressful!

- Motivate yourself to answer each question as effectively as you can.

- Work systematically through all the questions in the relevant section. You need to attempt every question: do not cherry pick or randomly select questions. The reason for this is simple. You need to identify whether there are specific types of questions where your performance would benefit from further practice.

brilliant tip

If you finish earlier than you expected then – just as you would in the real test – use this extra time as an ideal opportunity to go back and double-check any questions you were unsure about.

After taking a practice test

● Set aside a time when you will not be interrupted.

● Circle any incorrect answers.

● Go through each answer explanation for those questions you got wrong.

---

review your progress regularly

It is really important to review your progress regularly. Reflect upon the way you completed the practice test – as well as your overall performance. Focus on how you can avoid making the same mistake again. Try highlighting the answer explanations that you found most useful so you can review them again and again. If you do this just before your next practice session it will help instil the correct way of working in your mind.

Progress review

When you review your performance, ask yourself the following questions:

● How many questions did I get right?

● How many questions did I get wrong?

● If this is not your first practice session – Have I improved?

● What have I learnt?

● Are there particular types of question that I get wrong?

● Is there one specific thing that the answer explanation taught me? Have I applied this learning point correctly the next time around?

brilliant tip

It may be the last thing you want to do after taking the actual test, but on your test day you should also reflect on what – if any – questions you struggled with. This will help you target improvement areas if you face another verbal reasoning test.

Common concerns

If you are feeling apprehensive about your test take comfort from knowing that you are not alone – many people find the prospect of sitting a test quite daunting. Let's look at a few common concerns.

Help! I don't have much time

Ideally you will have sufficient time to plan your practice sessions over a period of several weeks as many test-taking strategies take time to develop. For readers with very limited time to get ready, the first priority is to complete those practice questions most relevant to you in Part 2. This will prepare you for what to expect and improve your overall confidence. Then read the strategic tips on test taking in Chapter 3.

Sample timetables

If you have 1 day ...

Read through the tactics and techniques in Chapter 3. Spend as much time as you can familiarising yourself with your test format, using the relevant chapter in Part 2.

If you have 1 week ...

Plan at least two practice sessions and start with the most relevant questions in Part 2. The chapters in Part 2 increase in difficulty level, so move backwards or forwards through Part 2 depending on whether you need to build your confidence with easier questions or challenge yourself with tougher questions. In addition to the test-taking tactics in Chapter 3 there are tips and strategies throughout all the chapters. Reading and applying these will help improve your overall speed and accuracy so it is worth scanning every chapter for tips.

If you have 1 month ...

Follow the above plan, but schedule in regular (at least bi-weekly) practice sessions over the course of the month, taking care to review and learn from the answer explanations. Each chapter in Part 2 has an Additional Resources box, which suggests online practice testing sites. If time permits, try taking these online practice tests.

If you have more than 1 month …

As with the above plan, you'll want to get as much practice as you can with your test format and learn to apply as many tips and tactics as you can. As time is on your side, check out the everyday practice suggestions in Chapter 5. These aren't miracle ways to enhance your performance overnight, but they are great techniques for improving your vocabulary and verbal reasoning skills in the longer term.

I'm having trouble getting started

Has your test preparation ground to a halt? Or maybe you haven't even managed to get started yet. Why not try a SWOT analysis to show how far you have come already and where you need to go. A SWOT analysis is a tool often used in business for strategic planning. This might sound intimidating, but it is really just a list. Four lists, in fact: **S**trengths; **W**eaknesses; **O**pportunities; **T**hreats. For example, the threat of failing the test if you don't start practising soon!

> try a SWOT analysis to show how far you have come and where you need to go

Here is an example of a SWOT analysis. Do any of these apply to you?

Strengths:

- You've bought this book with the intention of reading it and improving.
- You already have some skill in verbal reasoning otherwise you wouldn't be able to communicate with other people.
- Time is on your side. Don't waste a second more – start practising right away.

Weaknesses:

- There is one section of the test that you are dreading. There you go – focus your efforts on that area now.
- At school, English was your worst subject. As this book will show, verbal reasoning test formats are not necessarily like those you took at school – so don't despair.

Opportunities:

● You use your verbal reasoning skills every time you communicate. There are many ways to turn everyday situations into practice opportunities.

● Turn off the television in the evening or at weekends. Use that time to practise instead.

● Set aside your lunch break to practise, or get up half an hour earlier if you work best in the morning.

● Try using new words as you learn them in order to retain them in your memory. Just improving your vocabulary will have a positive impact on your verbal reasoning ability.

Threats:

● You don't spend enough time preparing in advance.

● You tend to procrastinate, or get easily distracted.

● You haven't kept up with your initial commitment to do as much as preparation as possible. Add your practice sessions to your diary – formalising your practice schedule will make it harder to skip practising.

● It has been a long time since you took a test. If that's your situation, use this book to get back into test-taking mode. The practice tests will help you refresh your skills and improve your test-taking technique.

How do I know if I am improving?

Effective feedback is the key to improving your overall perform-ance. That means going through the answer explanations in detail. Keep a record of how many questions you get right. Try other practice sections or, after a period of time, attempt the same test questions again. Compare your performances so you can gauge your improvement over time.

But I'm no expert on this subject!

Verbal reasoning tests at graduate level and above often involve reading comprehension, whereby you read a passage of text and then answer questions about it. Don't worry if the subject matter in the passage is

Don't worry if the subject matter in the passage is unfamiliar

unfamiliar to you. Many of the passages you read will be about areas in which you have no interest or background knowledge. You don't need to keep reading the passage until you have digested every single point that it is making. Instead, you should focus on understanding the particular part of the passage that a question refers to. Nor do you need to apply any outside knowledge of the subject. Remember that your answer must be based solely on the information presented in the passage. Don't let your answer be clouded by any background knowledge that you may bring to bear on the question. A reading comprehension task requires you to extract the relevant information to answer each question. Each question will relate to a particular part, or parts, of the passage. You will need to ferret out smaller pieces of information contained somewhere within the passage to answer the question correctly.

brilliant tip

You won't be asked to repeat information in exactly the same way as you read it in the passage. Understanding what is being asked is just one of the ways that your verbal reasoning is being assessed.

Where do I need to improve most?

As you work your way through the practice questions in the next part of this book it's important to periodically reflect on your progress and performance. Ask yourself the following questions.

Am I working at a steady pace?

Most tests are timed and you need to cultivate a focused and alert approach. Your first priority is to work accurately as there's no benefit in getting questions wrong. But remember that the person sitting next to you could pass because they answered more questions than you did – even though they also got more questions wrong.

Am I avoiding careless mistakes?

If you find yourself making too many careless mistakes you clearly need to slow down. Yes, you need to work at a brisk pace, but the key is to find the fastest pace that allows you to get questions right. It is also essential to read every word of every question very, very carefully to avoid sloppy mistakes.

Are any patterns emerging?

Look for trends. Do you tend to make more mistakes at the beginning of your practice session? This could be a consequence of nerves. You need to work on achieving a high state of mental alertness immediately and giving the test 100 per cent focus as soon as you start work.

Are you making more mistakes near the end of your practice session? This could be because you are rushing the last few questions. You need to work steadily and maintain concentration throughout an entire test.

I'm not getting any better

Are you clear on why you are getting questions wrong? This is key to improving – you need to learn from your mistakes. You may like to write down or highlight where you went wrong so that the next time you pick up this book you will be able to remind yourself. It's vital to know where you need to improve most. If you are unaccustomed to a particular type of question it makes sense to spend additional time getting comfortable with these questions. Don't assume that you can pass without learning how to do that sort of question.

The questions are too difficult for me

In order to improve your score you need representative questions that mirror the difficulty level of the real test. That is why the questions in the second part of this book are tailored to match the difficulty of your actual test. If you find your test questions too challenging, start with the practice questions in Chapter 7 and work your way up to the more difficult questions in subsequent chapters. Study the answer explanations so you can learn where you are going wrong.

✦ brilliant dos and don'ts recap

DO

✓ Practise right up to the day before you are going to be taking your test. Just as top tennis players practise their serve and strokes before each and every match, you need to keep practising for as long as you can.

✓ Study the format of the questions that you will be taking and focus your initial practice sessions on these questions.

✓ Continue practising with questions of a similar format and difficulty level. If you are comfortable doing more difficult questions, challenge yourself by working forwards in this book; attempt the preceding questions if you need practice with easier questions.

✓ Use all other opportunities for practice that come your way. Look up new words in the dictionary. Read the more difficult parts of the newspaper that you normally ignore or immediately throw away.

✓ Focus on understanding why you keep getting particular questions wrong and on avoiding any common mistakes.

DON'T

✗ Think that buying a more erudite newspaper, a dictionary (or even a thesaurus) is going to make an immediate difference. You need to use such tools proactively over a period of time.

✗ Just read the strategies and decide that that is exactly what you are going to do on the day – you will have forgotten them by then. To embed the strategies as part of your test-taking approach you need to apply them to the practice questions in this book.

✗ Don't think that merely improving your vocabulary will be sufficient to pass some of the more difficult verbal reasoning tests. Yes, you do need to understand all the words when reading a passage. But for certain tests you also need to be able to step back and to interpret what the passage or the paragraph as a whole is saying.

CHAPTER 3

Tactics and techniques

H as it been a while since you took a test? Are you panicking? If so, take a few deep breaths and stay calm. This chapter is packed with top tactics and techniques to help you get back into the swing of test taking and achieve the best results you can. In addition to measuring your verbal reasoning skills, the test you are about to sit will measure your ability to work under pressure. Fortunately there are lots of useful strategies that you can use on the big day and during your practice sessions.

Familiarise yourself

Knowing what to expect on your test day will give you a big advantage, so learn as much as you can about the test you are going to take. Your recruiting organisation may send

> learn as much as you can about the test you are going to take

you practice material in advance of your test. This may be in the form of sample questions, either online or in printed format. The information should also outline why the test is being used in the process and – most importantly – the exact nature of the test that you will be taking on the day. If you are taking the test online you should be provided with contacts for general queries as well as any technical questions relating to the operation of the online system.

This practice opportunity levels the playing field and gives everyone a fair chance – particularly important for people who have not taken a verbal reasoning test before. Make sure you use this material effectively so that you are comfortable with your test format. Ask questions in advance, particularly anything that is unclear in the test instructions. On the test day you will be given the opportunity to go through the administration instructions. But if this knowledge is already stored in your brain you will feel more comfortable about what you are going to be asked to do on test day.

brilliant tip

If practice material is not sent to you in advance, call your prospective employer and ask for any additional information regarding the test you are going to complete.

Practice strategies

Make sure you allow yourself plenty of time in advance of the real test to complete as many practice test sessions as possible. Continually review what you have learnt from previous practice test sessions so that you use your time most effectively.

Multiple practice sessions

I'd strongly advise against doing all your preparation in one huge hit. You will learn and retain much more if you undertake several practice sessions instead of one big one. At first it may seem as if you are only making small gains, but these small gains will soon add up to improved verbal reasoning skills.

Concentration

'Concentrate all your thoughts upon the work at hand. The sun's rays do not burn until brought to a focus.' So said the inventor

Alexander Graham Bell, and his words certainly apply to your task here. In order to answer questions accurately, you need to concentrate throughout your practice sessions and during the test itself. This is easier said than done – but concentration is vital if you want your brain to function at a high level. You can take measures to improve your concentration by getting enough rest and working in an environment free from distractions.

> concentration is vital if you want your brain to function at a high level

Take a break

Research has shown that most people's concentration levels drop off after spending longer than 40–50 minutes in any one practice session. You should plan your practice sessions accordingly. Also, if you start to lose concentration take a short break (of at least a few minutes) and come back to this book later. You'll hopefully come back feeling more focused after making a cup of tea. I know I do!

Learn from your mistakes

Take heed of any errors that you make throughout your practice session. Make a mental note of where you went wrong so you can avoid making similar mistakes in future. It's all too easy to mess up when when you are under pressure to perform.

Stretch yourself

Run through as many practice questions as possible in advance in order to challenge yourself mentally. Don't just focus on those practice questions that you can do quite easily – stretch yourself with harder questions. Undertake timed practice tests on a regular basis to get your brain used to working under pressure.

> stretch yourself with harder questions

You might be tempted to review the answers without doing the practice questions yourself. This might seem like a quick win, but it isn't. It will save you the time needed to work your way through the questions but it *won't* improve your verbal reasoning skills.

Timekeeping techniques

how you use your time during the test is important

It is essential to manage your time efficiently in the run-up to the test to ensure you fit in enough practice sessions. But how you use your time *during* the test is also extremely important. You don't want to be a 'hare' by working too fast, and you certainly don't want to be a 'tortoise' either. Neither of them wins when it comes to taking verbal reasoning tests. You don't necessarily need to finish the test in order to pass, but you do need a certain number of correct answers, so it is essential to pace yourself. Aim to spend a sufficient amount of time on each question. That's the maximum amount of time that you need to spend in order to get the question correct. No more and no less.

You are not necessarily expected to finish the test: you certainly don't need to finish it to pass if you get a high number of correct answers. But remember that you will be working under strictly timed exam conditions – as you had to do for school exams. You need a motivated, energised approach so that you can achieve the highest possible score.. If you consider your normal working pace a walk, you should be jogging briskly when you do the test! Right at the start of the test work out roughly how long you should be spending on each question. Try to ensure that you do not spend longer than this as you go through each question. To pace yourself you will need to keep an eye on the time remaining. Do a quick check roughly every 10 minutes; checking the time remaining against the number of questions that you have left to answer. If you have gone through practice questions you will have a good idea of the average time that you need to spend on each question.

Here are a few suggestions for pacing yourself.

- If you are working too fast then remind yourself that you must not make any careless mistakes.

- If you are going too slowly try to pick up speed – you need to complete as many questions as possible to do yourself justice.

- If you have time left at the end, go back to check your answers. Do not finish early – go back and double-check your answers if time permits!

brilliant tip

Buy a stopwatch and start timing your practice sessions to become more aware of your timekeeping. Challenge yourself to do more and more questions in each timed practice session to improve your speed.

Following instructions

Don't lose any marks for incorrect interpretation of information. Misreading the instructions is a very dangerous mistake to make. You must read each word very carefully. If you misinterpret the instructions you could answer several – if not all – questions incorrectly. The administrator is there to answer your questions. If something in the instructions is not what you are expecting or does not make sense to you then check with the

misreading a question
can cost you dearly

administrator before the test timer starts. You don't want to waste time during the test worrying about the instructions when you need to maximise the time you have to complete the questions themselves. Similarly, misreading a question can cost you dearly. I can't stress enough how essential it is to read each word of every question.

brilliant tip

Be sure to fill in your answer sheet *exactly* as instructed. For instance, if it asks you to shade in a circle, *don't* put a tick or cross in the circle. If your answer sheet is going to be scored by a computer, the machine will only be able to mark a standardised answer sheet.

Test-taking tactics

Remember that you are not expected to get a perfect score. Even if you get several answers wrong you can still pass the test, as long as a relatively small number of incorrect answers is outweighed by a much larger number of correct answers. Here are some top test-taking tactics to help you maximise your performance:

- Be methodical and do not jump ahead. Start by looking at the first question, answer it and then move on to the second. It is important to concentrate your mind on one question at a time.

- Use some intuition if you have a bad feeling about your answer. Just because there is a multiple choice option for it does not mean that it is the right answer. Rely on your intuition, too, if you can't decide between two answers.

Which was the first answer that you came to? Often it is best to stick with that answer.

- If you run out of time or you cannot answer some questions properly you have nothing to lose by putting down an educated guess. Two things to remember. You need to ensure that your test is not going to be negatively marked, which means that you would lose a mark for getting each question wrong. Secondly, you have three answer options – True, False, and Cannot Tell – so your chances of guessing correctly are one in three. That's not enough to pass!

- The questions are all worth the same amount of credit, so you should answer all the questions that you find easy first.

If you find that you are spending too long on a particular question don't get bogged down. It can be demotivating to spend a long time on one question and then find that you can't reach an answer or that your answer is not one of the multiple choice options. We all come across questions that we can't do, or just don't like the look of. Give your best guess and move on. Ensure that you have marked the question number so that you can go back at the end of the test if there is still time to finish it off. That said, you should only guess on questions that you have no possibility of answering correctly. Don't waste time. The quicker you decide to cut your losses the better since that will give you more time to work on the other questions that you may find easier to answer.

> only guess on questions that you have no possibility of answering correctly

brilliant tip

Remember that all questions are worth the same. No one cares if you leave a couple out. The important thing is to answer as many correctly as you can.

Stay positive

To maximise your chances of success you need to be able to concentrate 100 per cent on the test. A positive, confident mindset is also a necessity. Avoid letting any emotional factors distract or disturb you during the test. Try to maintain perspective. You don't need to get 100 per cent on the test – you just want to pass and do the best that you can. An optimistic attitude is key. Don't get bogged down by negative thinking or obsess about success or failure. Worrying is a waste of valuable energy. Instead, channel your energy in a positive way – by practising to improve your performance.

If you have completed plenty of practice questions, familiarised yourself with the test format, and learned how to apply the strategies in this book, you should be feeling confident. On the test day itself you need to get psyched up. Motivate yourself to work as quickly and as accurately as you can. It may sound like a tall order, but try to enjoy the challenge. Pump yourself up in advance – tell yourself to just do it!

Physical preparation

Mental preparation isn't enough – you need to prepare yourself for the test physically, too. Don't worry, you don't need to start doing push-ups or star jumps in addition to doing practice questions! You should just get a good night's sleep before the test. You will concentrate more effectively if you are fully rested. Worried that this might be difficult to achieve? Consider the night before as the final part of a successful test preparation process. If you've done your mental preparation in advance, you don't need to stay up all night 'cramming' – go for a walk, or watch a film, or have a relaxing bath – then turn in early.

Dealing with nerves

It is common for people who are unused to taking tests as part of a recruitment process to be quite anxious. Reflect on how you dealt with testing situations in the past. What helped you to stay calm previously? Put all your nervous energy to good use – doing extra practice is probably the best way to steady your nerves. If you believe that you are likely to suffer extreme stress on the day, you could benefit from learning some relaxation techniques.

While feeling a bit nervous is probably inevitable, there are measures you can take to ensure that you are as relaxed as possible on the day:

- Arrive with plenty of time to spare.
- Have everything that you will need with you, including such things as reading glasses and hearing aids if you need them.
- Take deep breaths and actually hold your breath for a couple of seconds before exhaling.

brilliant recap

As you have seen in this chapter, there are a lot of different strategies that you can apply to test taking in general and verbal reasoning questions specifically. If you want a quick and easy way to remember some key points, just think of the Three Big Cs:

- Concentration
- Continual practice
- Confidence

CHAPTER 4

Improving your reading comprehension

Many of the verbal reasoning tests featured in Chapters 9 and 10 have a reading comprehension format. This involves reading a passage of text and than answering questions associated with the passage. You probably remember doing a similar exercise at school. Once you have attempted a number of these questions you will get used to the format. However, remember that the most difficult reading comprehension questions won't ask you to repeat back information exactly the way you read it in the passage. The information that you need to answer the question is always contained within the passage, but the question may be phrased differently to the passage text. Understanding what is being asked is just one of the ways that your verbal reasoning is being assessed.

Learn the right steps

There is a knack to approaching these passage-based questions. It's bit like learning a dance routine. Just as learning to tango involves following a sequence of steps, applying certain steps to each question can improve your verbal reasoning test scores. So, let's dance!

applying certain steps to each question can improve your verbal reasoning test scores

For each passage you should ...

Step 1 Skim read the passage to get a rough idea of its content.

Step 2 Skim read the questions to get a rough idea of the level of difficulty and the sorts of things that you are going to be asked.

Steps 1 and 2 will prepare you for the level of complexity and the time that you need to spend answering the questions.

Read the passage again!

Step 3 Go through the passage again but read it more carefully this time. Do not spend time memorising the full details. Think in broad terms about the different areas that the passage is covering. At the same time try to make mental notes about where the specific pieces of information relating to each area are located in the passage.

Step 4 Try to get a broad sense of what you are going to be asked in each question and to know where this information was covered within the passage. Ask yourself: *Am I in a suitable position to answer the questions?* For more complex passages the answer to this will be no. Read the passage a third time. Try to identify the pieces of information in the passage that seem particularly important. Ask yourself the following broad questions as you read through:

- The introductory statement – What point(s) is/are being made here?
- The main body of the text – What does this explore/detail?
- The final statement(s) – What details are provided here?
- If there is a summary at the end of the passage, what point, if any, is it making?

Step 5 Ask yourself again: *Do I have a sufficient*

understanding to answer the set of questions? If the answer is yes, then you are ready to carefully read the first question. You may only need to read the passage in full twice if you already know where to find the relevant information.

brilliant tip

Remember that the passage will always be there for reference so you don't need to memorise its entire contents.

You need to follow the line of reasoning of each passage. What are the individual points that the author is making? What themes are coming out? Is an overall case being made? Are both sides of an argument given, together with a summary conclusion? But don't spend too long thinking about your own views on the subject matter itself. Your answer must be based only on the information that has been presented to you in the question, so don't let your concentration be drawn to the actual arguments and possible inaccuracies in the passage's information.

brilliant tip

It is important to remain objective rather than letting your own opinions – or knowledge – influence the way you answer a question.

Understanding the answer options

Many passage-based comprehension tests have three answer options: True, False and Cannot tell. Sounds obvious enough, right? Actually, it is surprisingly easy to get confused – especially about Cannot tell – so let's just review what each option means.

True means the statement is true *or* that it follows logically from the information given in the passage.

False means the statement is false – based only on the information given in the passage.

Cannot tell means you cannot say whether it is true or false because there is insufficient information given in the passage.

your answer must be based on the information given in the passage

Remember that your answer must be based on the information given in the passage alone. If the test format has different answer options for each question then you must read through *all* the answer options to find the one that most closely answers the question. Be wary of selecting the first answer that seems true – or right – to you.

The microscope technique

One helpful way to approach a passage is to imagine yourself using a microscope or camera lens. You start with a wide setting to look at the whole passage and then the questions. This gives you a broad picture, or a general understanding of what's in the passage. If you find this difficult to do, then try writing out the main theme or themes of passages before answering the questions. There won't be time to do this in an actual test situation but it's a good technique for training you to think about the big picture. Now focus the microscope (or camera lens) onto a specific part of the passage. For each question you need to zoom in to a specific part of the passage to get the detail that you need. If you know which part of the passage the question is asking about you are already well on your way to answering the question. You know where to find the vital clues.

> **brilliant** tip
>
> The passage may look very long to you but don't be put off by this. You may not even have questions relating to every sentence in the passage. Concentrate on examining the key sentences in as much depth as possible.

Key words

Watch out for certain key words and phrases in either the passage or question (or both!). These key words often act as the link between different pieces of information. In many cases they qualify the information that has been given. When you come across key words in passages and questions you need to focus on their precise meanings. You are being tested on reinterpreting the passage so ask yourself: do the key words have *exactly* the same emphasis in both the passage and question?

1. Contrast words

Contrast words and phrases (e.g. *however, although, but, alternatively, whereas, despite, rather, unless, instead, while, nevertheless, on the other hand, on the contrary, yet, at the same time, conversely*) are used to highlight differences. Contrast words make a transition between two clauses, or parts of a sentence, and emphasise a contrast in ideas or information.

Example

*Spain has always been a popular tourist destination, **however** it now faces competition from cheaper resorts in other countries.*

You need to pay careful attention to the information that follows the contrast word as it is often the key to answering the question.

Is the answer to the following statement True, False, or Cannot tell: *Spain is unrivalled as a tourist destination.* The answer is False.

The sentence says that Spain has always been popular, but goes on to say that it now faces competition.

2. Propositions

There are certain words and phrases that you need to treat as propositions. Don't be misled into thinking that they are facts. These include the following: *claims, suggests, advocates, recommends, advises, offers, proposes, believe* and *considers*. Treat these words with caution as they indicate a subjective statement based on one person's opinions rather than absolute evidence.

Example
The author claims that his book will improve your verbal reasoning test performance.

Is the answer to the following statement True, False, or Cannot tell: *This book will improve your verbal reasoning test performance.*

Yes, there is a very good chance that this book will improve your performance if used properly, but this is not a fact so the answer has to be Cannot tell.

3. Comparisons

Be on the look-out for comparative adjectives. These are words that compare two or more things. At the simplest level, these are superlatives such as *most, highest, biggest* and *least*. But there are other words for making comparisons, e.g. *more, lower* and *less*.

Example
*There is **less** unemployment in the UK today than at any other point in the past decade.*

If asked whether the following statement is True or False – *Unemployment rates are currently lower than they were five years ago* – the answer would be True. If there is *less* unemployment today than at any point over the past ten years, then it follows that unemployment rates are lower than they were five years ago.

4. Absolutes and generalisations

Adverbs such as *never* or *always* compare how frequently something occurs. Be alert for any words that imply something absolute, such as *no, never, none, always, every, entire, unique, sole, all, maximum, minimum* and *only*. Don't confuse them with generalisations, such as *many, almost always, some, nearly, usually, seldom, regularly, generally, frequently, typically, ordinarily, as a rule, commonly,* and *sometimes.* These generalisations create something of a grey area where a fact only applies some of the time. This is an important distinction. Just because something *usually* happens does not mean you can assume it *always* happens. It is important to recognise these words and interpret them accurately. Some words are relatively low generalisations, such as 'a few', 'a little', and 'only some'. Similarly, 'unlikely' and 'infrequent' tell you that there is still a slight chance, which is not the same as 'impossible'.

Example
*Most educators agree that excessive television viewing **usually** damages a child's concentration.*

If faced with the statement: *Excessive television always damages a child's concentration* you might be tempted to answer True. The answer is in fact False – because the word *usually* tells you that this is a high possibility, not a guaranteed effect.

So, to summarise: don't assume that *usually* means the same as *always*. In the world of verbal reasoning tests such words are miles apart!

brilliant tip

You need to look out for questions involving absolutes (All educators ...) and generalisations (Many educators ...).

5. Cause and effect

After doing lots of practice tests you will come to recognise cause and effect words and phrases. These include: *since, because, for, so, consequently, as a result, thus, therefore, due to* and *hence*. It is a good idea to focus on these as often a question will ask you to interpret how these words have been used to link different aspects of an issue or argument together. There are subtle differences between these words and phrases, as some signal stronger causal relationships than others. A word like *because* indicates a direct causal link. The word *so* also joins facts together but does not necessarily mean that it was the first fact that led to the second.

Examples
Consider the following two examples:

1   **As a result** *of oversubscription, Adam did not get a place on the philosophy course.*

2   *The philosophy course was oversubscribed* **so** *Adam enrolled in a different class.*

What is the answer if you are asked: *Did Adam get a place on the philosophy course?* In the first sentence, you know that he did not. The second sentence is more ambiguous. Perhaps Adam got a place, but opted out of the overcrowded course.

Be careful not to mix up causal words with words such as *then, next, after* and *later*. These words indicate a chronological sequence rather than a causal effect. For example, *then* does not imply that one thing caused another to happen, only that it happened after.

6. Speculation

Look out for words or phrases indicating speculation, such as *perhaps, probably, possibly* and *maybe*. Words such as *may, might* and *can* also point to the possibility of something happening.

You need to tread carefully with such phrases – they do not mean the suggested outcome is guaranteed, only that it is a possibility.

Example

If you are told – *The team is almost certain to win the championship* – you should not interpret this as meaning that the team will *definitely* win. It is just speculation, even if there are good reasons for making that prediction.

7. Addition

A question may ask you to add something up, for example, the number of options or a number of instances. Stay on the alert for any addition words and phrases, such as *also, again, in addition, as well as, besides, coupled with, alternatively, moreover* and *furthermore*. Also, be sure to look for more options or instances appearing later in a passage.

Example

Conglomerate Plc announced redundancies in its accounts team, as well as job losses in its logistics and human resources departments.

You may be asked to say whether the following statement is True or False: *Conglomerate Plc made redundancies in three parts of its business.* The answer would be True because the statement mentions job losses in accounts, logistics and human resources.

brilliant warning

Have you ever heard the saying 'Don't assume – it makes an ass out of you (u) and me'? Making incorrect assumptions is certainly a mistake in a verbal reasoning test!

Critical reasoning tests

Your test might not be called a reading comprehension test – it might be called a critical reasoning test. For all intents and purposes, this is the same type of test as an advanced verbal reasoning test and requires the same approach. Senior managers and executives who are going to be tested on their critical verbal reasoning can apply many of the skills and strategies described previously in this chapter. Don't get too hung up on whether or not yours is a critical reasoning test. Critical reasoning involves, quite literally, applying critical analysis to verbal information. When taking a critical reasoning test you need to analyse each passage with a critical eye. What logical conclusions can you draw? What assumptions have been made? How valid is that inference? What are the consequences?

> you need to analyse each passage with a critical eye

Many professions require critical reasoning skills – so that informed decisions can be made on the basis of the information available. Lawyers, for example, need to have strong critical reasoning skills. They need to be able to assess complex written and oral evidence. They also need to be able to communicate clearly their own interpretation of the evidence. It is essential for lawyers to be able to detect and make allowances for very subtle verbal nuances and differences in meaning.

A critical reasoning test has the same format as other passage-based verbal reasoning tests. The main difference is that the passages are more complex, with longer sentences and more unusual words. The difficulty level of the test that you have been asked to take will match the role or profession that you are applying for. The language and the verbal reasoning level of the test will be equivalent to what is expected for the role or profession.

When preparing for a critical reasoning test you should be aware of the following:

● You need to be very careful when interpreting the meaning of complex words, particularly when you are being asked to make a judgement on the basis of a shade of meaning.

● The passage may focus on a single argument, but it is also likely that it could contain more than one argument.

● In a critical verbal reasoning test there are likely to be ambiguities that you need to think through logically.

brilliant tip

If you are struggling to understand complex information, try writing your own questions based on the passage. This is a good technique to help turn things around.

Critical reasoning can be improved through practice and learning. See Chapter 5 for some great ways to improve your skills.

brilliant recap

● Approach passage-based questions in a systematic way so that you follow the line of reasoning.

● Be sure you understand the answer options.

● Answer the questions based only on information given in the passage.

● Look out for key words and phrases – they are often vital to interpreting the passage and answering the questions.

● A critical reasoning test is a type of advanced verbal reasoning test.

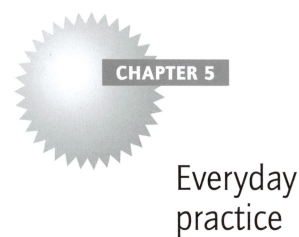

CHAPTER 5

Everyday practice

Although the practice test questions in Part 2 are the best way to practise, there are many other ways that you can turn everyday life into practice oppor-

> there are many other ways that you can turn everyday life into practice opportunities

tunities. If you have the time and are motivated to get more practice . . . good on you! Applying some – or all – of the suggestions in this chapter will not only boost your verbal reasoning skills but also introduce you to a wider range of reading materials and help you cultivate a richer vocabulary.

How to improve your reading comprehension

Maybe you realise that you need to speed up when reading complex passages or perhaps you want to get better at extracting the key themes from a short text. Whatever your reason, here are some great ways that you can incorporate practising your reading comprehension into your daily routine.

1 Read a daily newspaper. If you already do this then go up a level, choosing a newspaper at a higher reading difficulty level than your usual choice. Keep this as your regular choice of paper, at least until after your test session.

2 When you come across long paragraphs about complex subjects don't immediately move on to the sports or entertainment sections. Spend time reviewing the passages.

Ask yourself the following questions: What is the main point of each paragraph? Are both sides of an argument presented? What conclusion, if any, does the article come to?

3 If you usually avoid the opinion and comment pages of broadsheets or magazines then give them a go. These sections often contain challenging debates on popular subjects that require you to run through the pros and cons of an issue. Pay particular attention to the detail and the summary conclusion.

4 Visit your local library and select a range of books from different sections, especially the non-fiction shelves. Biographies, business books and technical titles will provide you with a broad range of reading material, just as the test questions will be drawn from a wide spectrum of topics. Don't bite off more that you can chew on your first visit. If you have time you can keep revisiting the library, upgrading to more challenging reading material each time that you visit.

reading different writing styles will help you practise interpreting complex verbal passages

As you can see from the suggestions above, reading a range of different writing styles will help you practise interpreting the sort of complex verbal passages that you are likely to find on your test. Getting comfortable with this level of text should enable you to approach the test day with the highest possible level of confidence.

brilliant tip

The key is to choose reading material of an equivalent level to that of the verbal reasoning test you will be taking. For graduates and senior managers, this means reading plenty of articles and books packed with long sentences and facts.

How to improve your vocabulary

The English language is incredibly rich. The *Oxford English Dictionary* contains over half a million words, but it is estimated that the average educated person only knows about twenty thousand of those. Clearly, we could all do with improving our vocabulary! If you want to improve your vocabulary in advance of your test, try some or all of the following:

- Keep track of any unfamiliar words that you read or hear. Carry a small notebook and jot these down so that later you can look up the definition online or in a dictionary. Say the word out loud so you master its pronunciation. Try using it in a sentence later that day – it will help you to remember the word.

- If you are really keen, once you have committed a new word to your memory, try to think of its synonyms and antonyms. These are words that mean the same (synonyms) and the opposite (antonyms). A thesaurus is a great tool to help you with this.

- Did you know that an eight-year-old child learns over three thousand new words a year, whereas an adult only learns on average twenty new words a day? So get down with the kids – use the same technique they use. Try to infer the meaning of the word from the context it is used in, and failing that *ask* the person who used it what it meant. Kids aren't self-conscious about doing this, and nor should you be.

- Read a wide range of materials, from newspapers and magazines to novels and non-fiction. Challenge yourself with something outside of your comfort zone – if fashion magazines are your thing, try *The Economist*.

- Be nosy! Talk to people from all walks of life. Ask them about their culture, their career, their hobbies and their interests. If they use a word you do not know, ask them what it means. You're much more likely to remember a word that you can relate back to a social situation. Seek out conversation with individuals who have a rich vocabulary. If you are brave enough, ask them to correct any mistakes in your own use of words.

- Play games. Expanding your vocabulary needn't be a chore – crosswords and word games such as Scrabble and Boggle are great ways to have fun while you learn.

brilliant tip

Building your vocabulary will have the knock-on effect of improving your reading comprehension skills.

How to improve your critical thinking

Improving your critical thinking skills is no small task. Critical thinking is the process of understanding and interpreting information in a logical way. It is not, as the name might imply, about thinking 'negatively'. Whether you are aware of it or not, you use your critical thinking skills every time you weigh up pros and cons and make a judgement call. Good critical thinking requires you to separate subjective opinions from objective facts. In a nutshell, you use your critical thinking skills every time you make a reasoned judgement call. As recommended in relation to improving your reading comprehension, it is important to practise reading a wide range of material. But if you want to improve your critical thinking skills you will need to evaluate the text in a deliberate, detailed and, above all, questioning manner.

critical thinking requires you to separate subjective opinions from objective facts

1   Visit the websites of broadsheet newspapers or television news stations. Most of these will have online forums that

enourage readers to post their views. Read the online news articles – focus on weighty subjects such as politics and finance – and then read the commentary posted both by punters and professionals. Think critically about all of the points being made – are they reasoned arguments based on fact or subjective opinions? If you are feeling inspired, join in the debate, using precise language and making a clear, well-justified point. Otherwise writing your own summary is a useful way to learn.

2   Read the review sections from weekend newspapers. Use two different-coloured highlighter pens to mark the words and phrases that are being used to make positive and negative arguments. How clear are the views being expressed? What objective evidence is being used to argue the case? Can you summarise the arguments? This extra engagement with the text will encourage you to read in a more active and concentrated fashion.

3   Ask questions. This sounds simple enough, but in fact most of us don't bother to question what we read and hear. Instead we make the mistake of treating biased opinions as fact. Train yourself to think open-mindedly and question everything as you interpret it.

4   Engage in discussion and debate with your friends and family. When sitting in a pub or café, bring up a controversial topic from the news and debate it with your companion. Don't just go with your gut feelings – try to make a logical, reasoned argument and support it with evidence. Think carefully about what the other person is saying: do you agree with or reject the other person's claims? Why?

5   Practise analysing what you hear – e.g. debates on the radio or on television or the speeches of politicians and other high-profile public figures. Play devil's advocate – try

formulating a contrary argument, regardless of your personal views.

brilliant recap

- There are many everyday opportunities for you to enhance your verbal reasoning skills.

- Take every opportunity that you can. Just think: most of these ideas are free and will fit into your daily routine.

- Remember that life goes on after your test and extensive practice could improve your reading comprehension for the rest of your life!

CHAPTER 6

What else do I
need to know?

irst, take a moment to consider how far you've come since the first time you picked up this book. Reflecting on the progress you have made should give your confidence a boost. Go on, give yourself a pat on the back! You've learned many useful test-taking strategies; it is nearly time to put them in action. But before that, let's have a look at the test process in general. Being fully aware of what to expect on your test day will help allay any jitters.

> let's have a look at the test process in general

What will I be told in advance?

You should have been provided with the following information, in keeping with best practice:

- logistical information, such as directions about how to get to the test centre;
- advance notice that you will be taking a verbal reasoning test, including the length of time that the test will take to complete;
- an explanation of the testing process;
- the part that the test will play in the overall process, including who will have access to your results;
- any feedback arrangements.

don't hesitate to get in touch with the contact name that has been supplied

If you feel that anything has not been adequately explained to you, or if you are uncomfortable with any aspect of these issues, then don't hesitate to get in touch with the contact name that has been supplied. Remember that your prospective employer or place of study will want to ensure that you are treated fairly throughout the testing process. That means from the time when you are notified that you need to undertake a verbal reasoning test right up to the time that you find out the outcome.

brilliant tip

Don't make any assumptions – if anything is unclear check before proceeding. The administrator is there to answer your questions.

What does the test administrator do on the day?

the test session needs to be standardised

In order for the test results to be reliable and fair, the test session needs to be standardised. That means the onus is on the test administrator to make sure you do what you are supposed to do and follow all the instructions exactly. Ask them about anything that is not clear, particularly the practice questions. Make sure that everything is clear *before* the timer starts since you will not be allowed to ask any questions once the test has started.

Many test publishers and consultancy firms offer British Psychological Society-recognised courses for training test administrators to administer and score verbal reasoning tests in the UK. This maintains the professional standards for conducting group test sessions.

Everyone taking the test must do the following:

- Complete the practice questions at the start of the test (in the initial 10–20 minutes). The administrator will ensure that every applicant present at the session completes the practice questions. The administrator will go through any of the practice questions if you are unclear as to how an answer was arrived at.

- Start the test at exactly the same time. You need to follow the administration instructions to the letter. Do not start until you are told to do so.

- Stop working as soon as the test administration says that the test has finished.

brilliant warning

Just as you would not be late for an interview, you should not be late for a test. Don't assume that you can be fitted in at whatever time you arrive. Your testing time will have been scheduled in so there's probably someone using your computer before and after you.

How are my test results used?

Your prospective employer or place of study expects that there will be a range of test scores on the verbal reasoning test. That's why the test is being used in the first place – to differentiate between applicants in terms of their verbal reasoning ability.

A couple of comparisons are made:

1 Each individual's overall score is compared to those of a large group of hundreds – sometimes thousands – of similar applicants who have taken the same test before. This is the norm group – the normal range of scores that are typical of

the type of people who sit the test. This way, your individual score is given in a meaningful way for that particular test.

2 At the same time, there is a particular group of applicants who took the test around the same time as you did. The pass mark is also likely to be based on how these other applicants performed. It may go up or down depending upon the number of vacancies for a particular job or course or on the number of people who have applied.

Your verbal reasoning test will be used to screen out unsuitable applicants

Your verbal reasoning test may be one stage in a long recruitment process. It will be used to screen out unsuitable applicants who do not have the necessary level of verbal reasoning ability. This process is called a sifting out or deselection process.

brilliant tip

Few people achieve the maximum mark for this norm group. This reflects the fact that you are not necessarily expected to finish the test in the time available and are not expected to receive full marks.

How does online testing work?

The prevalence of online testing has increased dramatically over the last few years. The most obvious difference between this and a pencil-and-paper test is that you take the test on a computer. From the administrator's perspective, this presents some complications.

One of the main concerns with online testing is proving that the person who takes the test is the same person who has applied. For proof of identification reasons you may need to complete an online test at a special testing centre. If you complete the test in the comfort of your own home you will certainly be asked to use a log-in and password (delivered to you separately) and the chances are that you will also be asked to undertake a further test session at a subsequent date.

The British Psychological Society and the International Test commission guidelines on computer-based and internet-delivered testing list the following four types of testing environment:

1 Open mode – where there is no means of identifying who is taking the test. This could be a practice test website where you do not need to enter a user ID and password before proceeding.

2 Controlled mode – where the test is only available to known users who must request and receive a user ID and password before they can proceed any further.

3 Supervised mode – where a test administrator supervises the test session and authenticates the identity of every test-taker present.

4 Managed mode – this features an even higher level of human supervision, typically at a dedicated test centre that strictly controls the test-taking environment.

brilliant warning

Do not be tempted to cheat by getting someone else to do the test as you will be retested further on in the process!

Adaptive tests

Some online verbal reasoning tests are adaptive tests. These are complex and potentially difficult tests that can be used to differentiate between high-level graduate job roles. The simplest types of adaptive verbal reasoning tests are just different variants of the test at different difficulty levels. In more complex adaptive testing set-ups the questions deliberately adapt to how you are performing as you progress through the test. So, if you are doing well, you will find that the questions get progressively harder. This allows your verbal reasoning ability to be thoroughly tested until you reach the maximum level at which you can answer questions correctly and within the time constraints.

Tips for taking online tests

- Online tests that you complete at home allow you as much time as you like to read the instructions onscreen. Make sure that you are absolutely clear on what you are being asked to do as there is no administrator to answer your questions. Take as much time as you need – you won't be keeping anyone waiting.

- You'll be the only person in the room, but that doesn't mean that you control the time allowed on the test. Once you have started you need to complete the test in the allocated time. You can take a break whenever you need to but it will cost you valuable time.

- A well-designed online test will have been thoroughly tested to work on most computers. You should be told the PC specification and internet access requirements in advance. But if you do have an access problem at any stage, use the contact information provided onscreen or by the person who sent you the invitation.

- If you do not have internet access at home, be resourceful: think about alternative venues for taking the test. For example, you could complete the test on a relative's computer or at a local library. Your local internet café might be another option, though it will most likely be quite noisy.

● Just in case your computer is not behaving on the day, it makes sense not to leave taking the test to the last minute.

Will I get any feedback?

Feedback may take several forms and should always be provided to you. It is important to remember that it is your relative performance that has been measured – meaning how your performance compared to those of

> Feedback may take several forms and should always be provided

the large norm group that have taken the test before. You won't receive marks out of ten or a percentage score as you might expect. Instead, your feedback could be one of the following:

● A standardised score such as a percentile. This is similar to a percentage but a percentile of 60 per cent means that you did better than 60 per cent of the norm group.

● A band that compares you to the norm group – e.g. average or above average. Remember, the term 'average' refers to average within a group of people similar to you who have taken the test for similar reasons to yourself. Your results are not being compared to those of the general population. So, a 'slightly below average' or 'below average' grade doesn't mean that you are worse than everyone else in the general population.

brilliant tip

It is best practice in the testing industry to provide feedback. Request this if you are not offered it.

Ensuring fairness

If you have a disability, then be sure to inform your prospective employer or educational establishment in advance if you require any adaptations to the testing process. It is likely that you would have been asked this question on your application form. You may also have been asked to complete a separate equal opportunities or monitoring form. Let them know how you have approached testing in the past and what provisions need to be made to ensure that you have equal access to the verbal reasoning test. This includes the format of the test, the medium through which it is communicated, and how it is communicated Adaptations can be made to the verbal reasoning testing process whenever it is appropriate to do so, including an additional time allowance and having the questions delivered in Braille or large print.

How do I behave on the day?

Relax . . . Staying calm and positive is the best way to approach your test. If you've read this book you will have done plenty of practice questions and have many strategies to use.

brilliant recap

The test administrator is there to ensure that the process is standardised for fairness. They are also there to answer your questions before the timed test begins.

● When taking an online test – either at home or at a testing centre – there are certain considerations you should be aware of.

● Feedback should always be provided and can take different forms. It compares your performance to that of a norm group.

PART 1

Summary

Now you know what a verbal reasoning test entails and how best to prepare for taking one. Everyone uses verbal reasoning every time they speak, send an email or text message. So in some ways you are already being tested every day!

It's time to move on as soon as you can to the practice questions in the next section. Always remember the Three Big Cs (Concentration, Confidence and Continual practice). I'll quickly remind you about the many benefits associated with Continual practice:

1 The best way to practise is with practice questions that were designed to mirror your actual test format. Part 2 offers you the opportunity to do this, and also to extend your practice to other verbal reasoning test formats.

2 Practice will increase your confidence. This will help your focus and concentration levels during the test.

3 Practice will help you to develop your test-taking strategies. Remember to look out for key words and phrases.

4 Practice leads to a more efficient approach. Your aim is to make the most effective use of the available time – working at speed, but not at the expense of accuracy.

Since verbal reasoning is a skill that we use every day, also remember the many everyday opportunities for practising that I suggested. It's over to you now to devote as much time as you possibly can to working through Part 2. Keep at it!

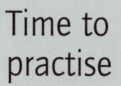

PART 2

Time to practise

Now it's time to put the strategies you learned in the previous chapters into action. This part of the book is all about practising. Here you can find examples of the most popular verbal reasoning tests used in Britain. Try to fit in as much practice as you possibly can before your test date. It is worth putting in the effort when acceptance into your future profession is at stake. In addition to the practice test questions, there are lots of Advice boxes scattered throughout this section. Be sure to read them, as they suggest great ways to improve your overall performance.

If you know your test format then you can go straight to the relevant chapter. For example, if you are preparing to take the UKCAT you should start by doing the UKCAT-specific practice questions. The following role-specific verbal reasoning tests have their own practice questions:

- Armed Forces (Chapter 7)
  - Army
  - Navy
  - RAF
- Qualified Teacher Status (Chapter 8)
  - Spelling
  - Punctuation
  - Grammar
  - Comprehension

- The UK Clinical Aptitude Test for Medical and Dental Degrees (UKCAT) (Chapter 9)

Other readers may know only that they will be taking, say, a general graduate-level or a senior managerial-level verbal reasoning test. In this case, you should start with Chapter 10, which contains practice tests at that level of difficulty.

For each test format there are many realistic practice questions mirroring the different types of questions that are likely to come up in the actual test. At the end of each chapter there are detailed, step-by-step answers for every question. Most of the practice questions are multiple choice. This doesn't make the questions easier. It doesn't mean that your test is 'multiple guess' either. Having written many such tests myself I can assure you that guessing is not an effective strategy.

If you don't know your test format, choose a format that most closely resembles the difficulty level. If you are a beginner I suggest you start with the next chapter and work through as many of the subsequent chapters as you can. Be selective if you like and dip into other practice chapters. You'll find a summary of what each test assesses at the start of each chapter. For example, if you want more practice at reading comprehension you can cherry-pick questions from several different chapters – from the QTS section onwards.

A note about difficulty levels

The questions in the following chapters appear in a rough order of increasingly difficulty – from the most basic to the most difficult. If the practice questions you started with are too difficult you can always go back to complete the earlier chapters. Equally, feel free to skip ahead if you find the questions too easy! Stretch yourself by trying the practice tests in subsequent chapters – these harder questions will help sharpen your verbal reasoning skills.

The Armed Forces entrance tests in the next chapter are examples of basic literacy tests. If you know that you are facing a basic literacy test you can use these tests as practice. By basic literacy I mean the ability to construct sentences and to understand the meaning of individual words. Tests of basic literacy may involve finding the most suitable replacement for a missing word in a passage or selecting a word that is opposite in meaning to the one shown.

More complex verbal reasoning tests build on this basic literacy and require you to understand the meaning of more unusual words. You may need to summarise the content of a passage or fill in a missing word in a sentence. The literacy test for achieving Qualified Teacher Status, for example, tests the use of grammar and punctuation when constructing sentences. The QTS practice tests can be used by anyone preparing to face a mid-level verbal reasoning test.

The most advanced verbal reasoning tests are those aimed at graduates and individuals applying for managerial or senior managerial level positions. Although there are many different tests in common use, they all use a passage-based format, where you read a short text and answer related questions. If you know that you are taking a passage-based test you can practise with questions in the graduate and senior managerial chapter, as well as the more difficult examples from the UKCAT and QTS comprehension sections.

CHAPTER 7

The Armed Forces

I t takes more than a willingness to serve your country to enlist in the British Armed Forces. In addition to demonstrating your physical fitness and proof of British residency, you must also take aptitude tests in order to be eligible to join the Army, the Royal Navy or the RAF. In today's increasingly technology-dominated world it is essential for military personnel to have literacy skills. Without a basic level of literacy, soldiers cannot comprehend documents and carry out their day-to-day duties competently. In order to ensure that recruits possess the necessary skills, each of the Armed Forces includes a literacy test component. Each set of questions in the following section will be useful practice for candidates hoping to enter any of the Armed Forces.

The Army
The Army entrance tests

So you want 'to be the best'? All recruits to the British Army start by taking a computerised battery of five tests – the British Army Recruitment Battery (BARB). The BARB is a touch-screen test. It assesses the ability to analyse information accurately and logically. The BARB is not timed – the computer will adjust the number of questions as you go along based on how quickly you are answering them. It usually takes about 30 minutes to do the entire battery.

How is it used?

The results of the BARB provide the Army with useful information on an applicant's training requirements. A candidate's score on the BARB test, based on the number of correct answers and the time taken to complete it, is called their GTI (General Trainability Index). The BARB does not operate on a pass/fail basis. Rather, it identifies suitable career options. A higher score on the BARB ensures recruits a greater choice of career options.

What does it test?

The five tests comprising the BARB are: Reasoning; Letter checking; Number distance; Odd one out; and Symbol rotation. Three of these tests rely upon verbal reasoning skills to some extent – Letter checking, Reasoning and Odd one out – and a practice test for each of these follows.

Additional resources

The Government's directgov website contains useful information on the qualifications required and how to apply to join each of the armed forces. You can search your particular career interest at:

http://careersadvice.direct.gov.uk/helpwithyourcareer/jobprofiles

You can also visit the Army's website for more information: www.army.mod.uk/join

Army – Letter checking

Instructions

In each question, review the four sets of two letters. These appear as four columns. You need to count the number of pairs where the same letter is shown as a capital letter and a lower-case letter.

> ### ☼ brilliant tip
>
> Think of each question as four columns of two letters rather than
> two rows of four letters.

Practice questions

1) l   j   f   s
    Q   B   L   S
    A 0   B 1   C 2   D 3   E 4

2) h   k   e   p
    H   K   E   P
    A 0   B 1   C 2   D 3   E 4

3) v   m   a   e
    J   P   Y   I
    A 0   B 1   C 2   D 3   E 4

4) S   A   N   V
    y   a   k   x
    A 0   B 1   C 2   D 3   E 4

5) p   h   s   b
    F   H   S   Y
    A 0   B 1   C 2   D 3   E 4

6) Q   C   H   W
    q   c   y   k
    A 0   B 1   C 2   D 3   E 4

7) i   b   e   a
    B   B   R   A
    A 0   B 1   C 2   D 3   E 4

8) k   g   d   q
    K   G   D   Q
    A 0   B 1   C 2   D 3   E 4

9) N   B   C   Z
    m   b   c   z
    A 0   B 1   C 2   D 3   E 4

10) O   Y   R   W
    o   y   r   w
    A 0   B 1   C 2   D 3   E 4

11) K   T   P   C
    l   u   f   e
    A 0   B 1   C 2   D 3   E 4

12) x   f   v   h
    X   F   V   H
    A 0   B 1   C 2   D 3   E 4

13) m   j   n   h
    M   J   N   H
    A 0   B 1   C 2   D 3   E 4

14) t   h   i   l
    J   Y   C   D
    A 0   B 1   C 2   D 3   E 4

15) c   r   b   u
    N   X   Z   I
    A 0   B 1   C 2   D 3   E 4

16) O   L   Y   F
    o   n   y   f
    A 0   B 1   C 2   D 3   E 4

17) r   s   g   i
    J   S   G   I
    A 0   B 1   C 2   D 3   E 4

18) J   U   K   S
    g   u   k   p
    A 0   B 1   C 2   D 3   E 4

19)	K	T	F	Y	
	n	o	c	y	
	A 0	B 1	C 2	D 3	E 4

20)	x	g	z	j	
	X	G	V	J	
	A 0	B 1	C 2	D 3	E 4

21)	v	t	k	o	
	J	T	K	O	
	A 0	B 1	C 2	D 3	E 4

22)	E	H	E	K	
	l	h	s	g	
	A 0	B 1	C 2	D 3	E 4

23)	I	G	Q	L	
	i	y	z	c	
	A 0	B 1	C 2	D 3	E 4

24)	j	b	t	x	
	B	O	S	X	
	A 0	B 1	C 2	D 3	E 4

25)	p	b	u	d	
	B	D	U	T	
	A 0	B 1	C 2	D 3	E 4

The answers to this section are on page 121.

Army – Reasoning

Instructions

Read the sentence and then answer a question associated with it when it appears on the computer screen. When taking the actual test you will only see one sentence at a time on the computer screen. You will have to memorise the sentence in order to answer the question when it is presented on the next screen. This might be easier for you if you just remember the name of the 'winner' – i.e. the highest, the fastest and so on.

The first thing that you need to focus on is the word that connects the two people. In the first practice example below this is *faster*. The next thing that you need to do is to decide the direction of the comparison that is being made. In the first practice example it is *Peter* who is the *faster runner*. Once you have established this, answering the question is easy. *Peter* is the 'winner' so the answer to the question is Paul.

Practice questions

1)   Peter is a faster runner than Paul.
     Who is the slower runner?
     A Peter
     B Paul

2)   Raj has a more expensive watch than Jean.
     Who has the more expensive watch?
     A Raj
     B Jean

3)   Sally is better at football than Lisa.
     Who is the better footballer?
     A Sally
     B Lisa

4)   David is a faster typist than Pauline.
     Who is the slower typist?
     A David
     B Pauline

5)   Mohammed reads more books than Gene.
     Who reads less?
     A Mohammed
     B Gene

6) Siri is brighter than Penny.
   Who is brighter?
   A Siri
   B Penny

7) Stephen is a stronger swimmer than Sarah.
   Who is the weaker swimmer?
   A Stephen
   B Sarah

8) Philip is more talented than Roger.
   Who has less talent?
   A Philip
   B Roger

9) Graham is not as quick at maths as Harold.
   Who is slower at maths?
   A Graham
   B Harold

10) Alfred is quicker than Harry.
    Who is slower?
    A Alfred
    B Harry

11) Lisa is better at sports than Asha.
    Who is less good at sports?
    A Lisa
    B Asha

12) Vincent is not as good a cook as Gordon.
    Who is the better cook?
    A Vincent
    B Gordon

13) Jack is not as good a gardener as Nasim.
    Who is the lesser gardener?
    A Jack
    B Nasim

14) Ada is not as outgoing as Zack.
    Who is more outgoing?
    A Ada
    B Zack

15) Isaac is not as good a pool player as Peter.
    Who is the lesser pool player?
    A Isaac
    B Peter

16) Valery is not as strong a card player as Shoaib.
    Who is the better card player?
    A Valery
    B Shoaib

17) Evelyn is friendlier than Amritpal.
    Who is friendlier?
    A Evelyn
    B Amritpal

18) Richard is more academic than Freddy.
    Who is less academic?
    A Richard
    B Freddy

19) Riya is older than Andy.
    Who is younger?
    A Riya
    B Andy

20) Sarah has a smaller car than Jason.
    Who has the bigger car?
    A Sarah
    B Jason

21) Manuel has a lower drive than Yasar.
    Who has less motivation?
    A Manuel
    B Yasar

22) Gary earns more money than Malcolm.
   Who has a higher salary?
   A Gary
   B Malcolm

23) Raymond is less happy than Tarnjit.
   Who is sadder?
   A Raymond
   B Tarnjit

24) Chukwuma is faster than Dirk.
   Who is slower?
   A Chukwuma
   B Dirk

25) Patricia is less eager than Geoffrey.
   Who is keener?
   A Patricia
   B Geoffrey

The answers to this section are on pages 121–122.

Army – Odd one out

Instructions

Review the set of three words presented in each question. You need to determine which two words are connected. These two words could be connected because they mean the same thing, or almost the same thing, or because they mean the opposite thing. The answer is the third word – the odd one out. The first thing that you need to do is find the connection between two of the words. You might think that there are endless possibilities but most of the time the connection will be quite simple. Possible connections include being opposites (see practice question 2), belonging to the same category (see practice questions 12 and 24), or being synonyms (see practice question 22).

brilliant tip

Quickly and accurately work through as many of the questions as you possibly can. Don't make the mistake of going too slowly. Make a firm decision and avoid going back to double-check it.

Practice questions

1)   hat   man   woman
     A hat   B man   C woman

2)   cool   arm   hot
     A cool   B arm   C hot

3)   beer   wine   pull
     A beer   B wine   C pull

4)   queen   computer   king
     A queen   B computer   C king

5)   fist   last   first
     A fist   B last   C first

6)   diamond   good   bad
     A diamond   B good   C bad

7)   loud   heavy   quiet
     A loud   B heavy   C quiet

8)   five   whisper   eight
     A five   B whisper   C eight

9)   green   keeper   blue
     A green   B keeper   C blue

10)   boy   girl   baby
     A boy   B girl   C baby

11)   town   sweat   city
    A town   B sweat   C city

12)   goat   wing   cow
    A goat   B wing   C cow

13)   fair   name   unfair
    A fair   B name   C unfair

14)   lake   jumper   river
    A lake   B jumper   C river

15)   bungalow   beef   lamb
    A bungalow   B beef   C lamb

16)   sad   happy   jeep
    A sad   B happy   C jeep

17)   water   gift   present
    A water   B gift   C present

18)   right   enable   left
    A right   B enable   C left

19)   knife   attack   fork
    A knife   B attack   C fork

20)   bench   major   minor
    A bench   B major   C minor

21)   hard   event   soft
    A hard   B event   C soft

22)   same   identical   cash
    A same   B identical   C cash

23)   goal   target   gate
    A goal   B target   C gate

24)   steel   join   copper
    A steel   B join   C copper

| 25) | take | | prepared | | unprepared |
| | A take | B | prepared | C | unprepared |

The answers to this section are on pages 122–123.

The Royal Navy
The Standard Naval Entrance Test

The Standard Naval Entrance Test, or Recruiting Test (RT), is a battery of four multiple choice tests covering the following areas: reasoning, verbal ability, numeracy and mechanical comprehension. The test is completed in a paper-and-pencil format. Each sub-test is timed separately by a trained test adminstrator and the whole thing takes about an hour to complete.

This book provides practice questions for two of the RT sub-tests: verbal ability and the verbal portion of the reasoning test.

How is it used?

The Royal Navy's recruitment is a staged process. You must successfully complete one stage before you move on to the next. A successful performance in the RT means you will go on to have a selection interview. The pass mark for the test varies depending on which branch you are applying to – for example, the most technical branches will require a higher pass mark. But for many of the branches, a mark of 50 per cent is acceptable.

Additional resources

There is a very useful practice test booklet available on the official Royal Navy website. I highly recommended that you download it, read through the information and complete the additional practice questions. Visit

http://www.royalnavy.mod.uk/server/show/nav.6259

The government's directgov website contains useful information on the qualifications required and how to apply to join the Royal Navy if you search at:

http://careersadvice.direct.gov.uk/helpwithyourcareer/jobprofiles

Navy – Reasoning: what does it test?

The reasoning test has 30 questions and lasts nine minutes. It tests your ability to process information, identify relationships and differentiate between relevant and irrelevant information. The reasoning test features several different types of questions: numerical reasoning, spatial reasoning and abstract reasoning, as well as verbal reasoning. The practice questions below are only verbal reasoning questions, but in the actual test this type of question will appear alongside the other reasoning questions – i.e. numeracy, special and abstract reasoning.

Instructions

For each sentence that you are presented with, choose the correct word from the five multiple choice answer options. In the real test you will have a separate answer sheet on which to record your answers. You indicate the correct answer by crossing through that letter. Make sure that you only mark one answer per question. If you decide to change your answer, you blacken out your original answer then cross through the letter for your new answer.

Focus on working accurately while also trying to complete as many questions as you can. You need to be able to complete at least three questions per minute. Time yourself and see how close you are to achieving this benchmark. Try the other Armed Forces verbal reasoning questions to get additional practice.

> ### ✦ **brilliant** tips
>
> ● If you do not recognise a word then ask yourself whether it looks like any other words you know.
>
> ● If you are unsure of an answer, try to eliminate as many of the answer options as possible.

Practice questions

1) LUNCH is to EAT as BEVERAGE is to
   A CONSUME
   B DRINK
   C DROWN
   D SWALLOW
   E GLASS

2) TEPID means the same as . . .
   A WARM
   B HOT
   C COLD
   D BATH
   E WATER

3) FISHMONGER is to FISH as ESTATE AGENTS are to
   A SHOP
   B COD
   C HOUSES
   D ANGLE
   E RENT

4) COHERENT is the opposite of
   A AMBIGUOUS
   B ARTICULATE
   C VARIOUS
   D CONNECTED
   E RATIONAL

5) FEASIBLE is the opposite of
   A ACHIEVABLE
   B RATIONAL
   C IMPOSSIBLE
   D RISIBLE
   E EASY

6) PLANE is to PILOT as CAR is to
   A VEHICLE
   B DRIVER
   C PLAIN
   D AIRMAN
   E FLY

7) SIMPLE means the same as . . .
   A SAME
   B COMPLEX
   C CONFLICTING
   D EASY
   E FEASIBLE

8) REGULAR is the opposite of
   A FREQUENTLY
   B IRREGULAR
   C ALWAYS
   D UNIFORM
   E RECURRING

9) ROAD is to DRIVE as FOOTPATH is to
   A PASSAGE
   B ROUTE
   C FOREST
   D NAVIGATE
   E WALK

10) NOVEL means the same as
   A NEW
   B HOVEL
   C UNORIGINAL
   D UNEASY
   E SELDOM

11) EQUITABLE is the opposite of
   A ALIKE
   B DOUBLE
   C UNFAIR
   D UNIFORM
   E EQUITY

12) PEN is to WRITE as ERASER is to
   A DRAW
   B PENCIL
   C INK
   D ERASE
   E PAPER

13) OPERATE means the same as
   A USE
   B SURGEON
   C DISCLOSE
   D HOSPITAL
   E DIVEST

14) PLENTIFUL is the opposite of
   A MORE
   B BUMPER
   C BOUNTIFUL
   D SCARCE
   E UNLIKELY

15) JUDGE is to COURT as SAILOR is to
   A TAILOR
   B SEAMAN
   C LAWYER
   D MAGISTRATE
   E SHIP

16) SIMILAR means the same as
   A OPPOSITE
   B ADDITION
   C COMPARABLE
   D EXACT
   E DIVERGENT

17) RAPID is the opposite of
   A WATERFALL
   B FAST
   C VAPID
   D SPEEDILY
   E LEISURELY

18) THERMOMETER is to TEMPERATURE as WATCH is to
   A HOT
   B HOUR
   C TEMPERAMENT
   D TIME
   E LOOK

19) ENTIRE means the same as
   A COMPLETE
   B GLOBAL
   C FRACTION
   D ENTITY
   E PORTION

20) MEAN is the opposite of
   A EXACT
   B AVERAGE
   C GENEROUS
   D TIGHT
   E NASTY

The answers to this section are on page 123.

Navy – Verbal Ability: what does it test?

This verbal ability test assesses your ability to understand the meaning of words and the relationships between words. There are four different types of questions:

1   The first type of question gives you a short word and five other short words in brackets. The word outside the bracket will go with only four of the words inside the bracket to make longer words. The answer is the word it will not go with.

2   The second type of question gives you five words. The answer is the one word that describes or includes all the other words.

3   The third type of question gives you a sentence with a missing word. You must decide which word from the answer options best completes the sentence.

4   The fourth type of question gives you five sentences, four of which have the same meaning. The answer is the question that has a different meaning.

Instructions

There will be 30 questions to complete in nine minutes. In the real test you will have a separate answer sheet on which to record your answers. You indicate the correct answer by crossing through that letter. Make sure that you only mark one answer per question. If you decide to change your answer, you blacken out your original answer then cross through the letter for your new answer.

Practice questions

1) The word outside the brackets will go with only four of the words inside the bracket to make longer words. Which one word will it not go with?

	A	B	C	D	E
be	(long	sides	hind	fore	ween)

2) Which word has a meaning that extends to or includes the meaning of all the others?
   A beret
   B cap
   C hat
   D fedora
   E bowler

3) The sentence below has a word missing. Which one word makes the best sense of the sentence?
   The house has a great location, but it is so . . . that the buyer will need to renovate it completely before moving in.
   A dilapidated
   B modern
   C expensive
   D noisy
   E attractive

4) The word outside the brackets will go with only four of the words inside the bracket to make longer words. Which one word will it not go with?

	A	B	C	D	E
rest	(less	ion	ate	ore	rain)

5) Which word has a meaning that extends to or includes the meaning of all the others?

A semi-detached

B terraced

C detached

D house

E maisonette

6) Four of the five sentences have the same meaning. Which one sentence has a different meaning?

A I ate my dinner already.

B I have not yet eaten my dinner.

C My dinner has already been eaten.

D I have already eaten my dinner.

E The meal that I ate was dinner.

7) The word outside the brackets will go with only four of the words inside the brackets to make longer words. Which one word will it not go with?

	A	B	C	D	E
con	(tent	trite	verge	dam	sort)

8) Which word has a meaning that extends to or includes the meaning of all the others?

A dog

B goldfish

C pet

D cat

E horse

9) The sentence below has a word missing. Which one word makes the best sense of the sentence?

Even though she had won the lottery, Ellen remembered her poor childhood and remained . . . with her money.

A extravagant

B neat

C bold

D kind

E thrifty

10) The word outside the brackets will go with only four of the words inside the brackets to make longer words. Which one word will it not go with?

	A	B	C	D	E
super	(star	sonic	idea	vision	natural)

11) Which word has a meaning that extends to or includes the meaning of all the others?

A vehicle

B car

C van

D bus

E taxi

12) Four of the five sentences have the same meaning. Which one sentence has a different meaning?

A The boy walked his dog in the morning.

B Before school, the boy walked his pet dog.

C The boy's dog was taken for a walk first thing.

D The dog was walked this morning by the boy.

E The boy still needs to walk his dog.

13) The word outside the brackets will go with only four of the words inside the brackets to make longer words. Which one word will it not go with?

	A	B	C	D	E
at	(tic	one	test	tune	tong)

14) Which word has a meaning that extends to or includes the meaning of all the others?

A red

B colour

C orange

D yellow

E green

15) The sentence below has a word missing. Which one word makes the best sense of the sentence?

The famous chef, who had a fiery temperament, was as renowned for his blistering ... as for his exotic recipes.

A ingredients
B reviews
C outbursts
D saucepans
E ovens

16) The word outside the brackets will go with only four of the words inside the brackets to make longer words. Which one word will it not go with?

	A	B	C	D	E
an	(gel	them	tics	den	on)

17) Which word has a meaning that extends to or includes the meaning of all the others?

A florist
B chemist
C baker
D shop
E butcher

18) The word outside the brackets will go with only four of the words inside the brackets to make longer words. Which one word will it not go with?

	A	B	C	D	E
inter	(cede	man	pose	mingle	est)

19) Four of the five sentences have the same meaning. Which one sentence has a different meaning?

A The shop is only open at the weekend.
B At the weekend, the shop is not open.
C The shop is not open on Saturday or Sunday.
D Every weekend the shop is shut.
E The shop is closed at the weekend.

20) The word outside the brackets will go with only four of the words inside the brackets to make longer words. Which one word will it not go with?

	A	B	C	D	E
in	(apt	burn	form	bred	active)

21) Which word has a meaning that extends to or includes the meaning of all the others?

A table
B furniture
C chair
D sofa
E bureau

22) The sentence below has a word missing. Which one word makes the best sense of the sentence?

After getting such terrible reviews on their opening night, the play's cast lacked . . . as they prepared for the next show.

A concern
B tickets
C pity
D confidence
E drama

23) The word outside the brackets will go with only four of the words inside the brackets to make longer words. Which one word will it not go with?

	A	B	C	D	E
pass	(word	port	age	ion	eon)

24) Which word has a meaning that extends to or includes the meaning of all the others?

A flower
B daisy
C rose
D tulip
E daffodil

25) Four of the five sentences have the same meaning. Which one sentence has a different meaning?

A The weather continued to be cold and rainy.

B It is cold and wet outside.

C For the past few days, it has been cold and wet.

D Outside, the cold rain was falling.

E Tomorrow the weather will improve.

26) The word outside the brackets will go with only four of the words inside the brackets to make longer words. Which one word will it not go with?

	A	B	C	D	E
land	(scape	sort	slide	lord	mark)

27) Which word has a meaning that extends to or includes the meaning of all the others?

A potato

B carrot

C vegetable

D pea

E bean

28) Which word has a meaning that extends to or includes the meaning of all the others?

A apple

B chicken

C soup

D turkey

E food

29) Four of the five sentences have the same meaning. Which one sentence has a different meaning?

A Erica forgot to give Richard a birthday present.

B Richard did not receive a birthday present from Erica.

C Unfortunately, Erica had forgotten Richard's birthday present.

D Richard thanked Erica for the birthday present she gave him.

E Erica forgot to bring Richard's birthday present.

30) The word outside the brackets will go with only four of the words inside the brackets to make longer words. Which one word will it not go with?

	A	B	C	D	E
head	(age	first	room	phone	ache)

31) Which word has a meaning that extends to or includes the meaning of all the others?

A one
B five
C hundred
D number
E twenty

32) The sentence below has a word missing. Which one word makes the best sense of the sentence?

The scientist was normally very shy, but if you asked about his work he would become quite ... as he explained his experiments enthusiastically.

A reserved
B boring
C sincere
D animated
E rude

33) The word outside the brackets will go with only four of the words inside the brackets to make longer words. Which one word will it not go with?

	A	B	C	D	E
car	(go	ion	pet	mine	rot)

34) Which word has a meaning that extends to or includes the meaning of all the others?

A lawyer
B accountant
C profession
D doctor
E architect

35) Four of the five sentences have the same meaning. Which one sentence has a different meaning?

A Brian sold his stamp collection.

B Brian collects stamps.

C Brian has a stamp collection.

D The stamp collection belongs to Brian.

E The stamps have been collected by Brian.

36) The word outside the brackets will go with only four of the words inside the brackets to make longer words. Which one word will it not go with?

	A	B	C	D	E
am	(end	using	bush	steal	oral)

37) Which word has a meaning that extends to or includes the meaning of all the others?

A slipper

B shoe

C trainer

D tennis

E running

38) The sentence below has a word missing. Which one word makes the best sense of the sentence?

We would have been better off hiring a four-wheel drive, as the road through the mountains was winding and even more . . . in the snow.

A polluted

B scenic

C cold

D narrow

E dangerous

39) The word outside the brackets will go with only four of the words inside the brackets to make longer words. Which one word will it not go with?

	A	B	C	D	E
in	(deed	cur	bed	crease	corporate)

40) Which word has a meaning that extends to or includes the meaning of all the others?

A weather

B hot

C wet

D cold

E changeable

41) Four of the five sentences have the same meaning. Which one sentence has a different meaning?

A Fred made a cake for the fair.

B Fred bought a cake at the fair.

C At the fair, there was a cake made by Fred.

D Fred's cake was at the fair.

E A cake made by Fred was at the fair.

42) The word outside the brackets will go with only four of the words inside the brackets to make longer words. Which one word will it not go with?

	A	B	C	D	E
con	(sign	tail	tent	sent	fuse)

43) Which word has a meaning that extends to or includes the meaning of all the others?

A steel

B copper

C iron

D lead

E metal

44) The sentence below has a word missing. Which one word makes the best sense of the sentence?

When the clock struck midnight, the party's gracious hostess ... suggested that her guests should start heading home.

A cleverly

B softly

C wisely

D hurriedly

E tactfully

45) The word outside the brackets will go with only four of the words inside the brackets to make longer words. Which one word will it not go with?

	A	B	C	D	E
super	(vision	nil	market	intend	sonic)

46) Which word has a meaning that extends to or includes the meaning of all the others?

A trumpet

B instrument

C drum

D guitar

E flute

47) Four of the five sentences have the same meaning. Which one sentence has a different meaning?

A The teacher presented the pupil with the award.

B The pupil's award was given by the teacher.

C The pupil received the award from the teacher.

D The teacher was presented with an award by the pupil.

E The pupil won an award, which was presented by the teacher.

48) The word outside the brackets will go with only four of the words inside the brackets to make longer words. Which one word will it not go with?

	A	B	C	D	E
head	(light	way	stone	wind	fill)

49) Which word has a meaning that extends to or includes the meaning of all the others?

A book
B novel
C guide
D poetry
E biography

50) The sentence below has a word missing. Which one word makes the best sense of the sentence?

Historians have ... the mysterious rock formations at Stonehenge for generations, but remain uncertain about the ancient stones' original purpose.

A admired
B studied
C photographed
D visited
E enjoyed

51) The word outside the brackets will go with only four of the words inside the brackets to make longer words. Which one word will it not go with?

	A	B	C	D	E
inter	(view	lock	cede	lace	side)

52) Which word has a meaning that extends to or includes the meaning of all the others?

A apple
B pear
C fruit
D banana
E orange

53) Four of the five sentences have the same meaning. Which one sentence has a different meaning?

A My library book is due back today.

B Today is the day on which my library book is due back.

C My library book is now overdue.

D Today my library book is due back.

E I must take my book back to the library today.

54) The word outside the brackets will go with only four of the words inside the brackets to make longer words. Which one word will it not go with?

	A	B	C	D	E
super	(human	power	star	sonic	tend)

55) Which word has a meaning that extends to or includes the meaning of all the others?

A antelope

B giraffe

C lion

D animal

E zebra

56) The sentence below has a word missing. Which one word makes the best sense of the sentence?

Jane has bought a very ... new computer with a wide range of different programmes, even though she only really needs it for basic functions such as word processing and email.

A popular

B dependable

C sophisticated

D sleek

E heavy

57) Four of the five sentences have the same meaning. Which one sentence has a different meaning?

A We are going to the seaside for our holiday.

B The seaside is where we are going on holiday.

C Last year we went on holiday to the seaside.

D Our holiday will be spent at the seaside.

E We will be spending our holiday at the seaside.

58) Which word has a meaning that extends to or includes the meaning of all the others?

A plane

B chisel

C saw

D hammer

E tool

The answers to this section are on pages 124–125.

The Royal Air Force

Applying to the RAF is a process that takes several months from initial application through to acceptance. The staged selection process involves interviews, a fitness test and, of course, aptitude tests. The tests that you are asked to take will depend upon the particular RAF career that you are applying for: officer, non-commissioned aircrew or airman/airwoman. The section below aims to prepare you for the verbal reasoning component of the Airman Selection Test.

The RAF's Airman/Airwoman Selection Test

The RAF's Airman/Airwoman Selection Test (AST) is used as part of the process for becoming an airman/airwoman. The AST comprises the following seven multiple choice tests:

1 Verbal reasoning

2 Numerical reasoning

3 Work rate

4 Spatial reasoning

5 Electrical comprehension

6 Mechanical comprehension

7 Memory

How is it used?

If you pass the AST you will progress to the next recruitment stage – the health assessment.

Additional resources

There is a sample Airman/Airwoman Selection Test containing examples of each type of aptitude question at the following URL:

http://www.raf.mod.uk/careers/aptitude/aptitude.html

Additional information on the use of tests within the RAF selection procedure can be found at the official RAF website:

http://www.raf.mod.uk/careers/nextsteps/testsandinterviews.cfm

The Government's directgov website contains useful information on the role, the qualifications required and how to apply. Just search at:

http://careersadvice.direct.gov.uk/helpwithyourcareer/
jobprofiles/profiles

Instructions

You will be presented with an introductory passage. This passage comprises one to three sentences followed by a number of statements. Read the passage then decide which of the multiple choice options is correct – based only on the information presented to you in the passage. The real test has 20 questions and allows you 15 minutes to answer these. You need to be able to complete four questions on average every three minutes. Time yourself and see how close you are to achieving this benchmark.

brilliant tip

The previous practice questions have been testing basic literacy whereas the questions that follow are at a more advanced level. Try the other Armed Forces questions if you need to get additional practice before progressing on to the more difficult verbal reasoning questions below.

Practice questions

A group of teenagers are planning a Saturday night trip to the cinema. Their local multiplex has a range of different films showing across different film genres.

● Nicola likes science fiction or fantasy films best.

● Hifzu likes comedy films best. Hifzu will not go to see an action film.

● Carol likes thrillers, comedy and action films.

● Simon likes thrillers best.

● Peter will not go to see a romantic film.

1) What type of film would suit Simon and Carol most?
   A Romantic
   B Fantasy
   C Action
   D Thriller
   E Comedy

2) Whose first preference is to see a fantasy or science fiction film?
   A Peter
   B Nicola
   C Hifzu
   D Carol
   E Simon

3) The five teenagers want to go and see a film together. Which film genres are not an option?
   A Romance and action
   B Fantasy and romance
   C Action
   D Fantasy
   E Thriller and action

4) Who would like to go and see a comedy film?
   A Peter, Nicola
   B Hifzu, Simon
   C Hifzu, Carol
   D Peter, Carol
   E Simon, Nicola

5) Who would prefer to see a romantic film?
   A Peter
   B Nicola
   C Hifzu
   D Carol
   E Can't tell

Mr Phillips is the Managing Director of an IT company based in Salford. He has two Directors who report to him – Mrs Kaur and Mr Patel. Mrs Salamon is the Director of Operations. Mr Patel is the Client Director. Mrs Jenkins supports Mrs Salamon within the Operations team. Mr Hays is the Deputy Client Director and reports to Mr Patel. Mrs Jenkins is the only administrator who works for the company. Mr Phillips, Mr Patel, Mrs Salamon, Mrs Jenkins and Mr Hays are all graduates.

6) Who is best suited to completing administrative jobs?
   A Mr Phillips
   B Mrs Kaur
   C Mr Patel
   D Mrs Jenkins
   E Mr Hays

7) Who is the only non-graduate that works for the company?
   A Mr Phillips
   B Mrs Kaur
   C Mr Patel
   D Mrs Jenkins
   E Mr Hays

8) Who works with the Director of Operations?
   A Mr Phillips
   B Mrs Kaur
   C Mr Patel
   D Mrs Jenkins
   E Mr Hays

9) Who takes charge of client accounts when Mr Patel is away on holiday?
   A Mr Phillips
   B Mrs Kaur
   C Mr Patel
   D Mrs Jenkins
   E Mr Hays

10) Who is the most senior member of staff?
   A Mr Phillips
   B Mrs Kaur
   C Mr Patel
   D Mrs Jenkins
   E Mr Hays

A family is considering which of five popular tourist attractions to visit on Sunday afternoon:

- The Tithe Museum is expensive but is the adults' first choice.

- Penny Park is the only option within walking distance but has a poor reputation for litter and graffiti.

- Speedy's Fun Fair rides are overpriced according to the guidebook, but are always popular with children.

- Seacombe Beach is too far to drive in a day, but is accessible by public transport. It is the only option that has free entrance.

- The Peak National Monument has the highest number of star ratings in the family's guidebook, but the children are refusing to go there.

11) Which is the cheapest option?
   A Tithe Museum
   B Penny Park
   C Speedy's Fun Fair
   D Seacombe Beach
   E Peak National Monument

12) Which attraction is the easiest to walk to?
   A Tithe Museum
   B Penny Park
   C Speedy's Fun Fair
   D Seacombe Beach
   E Peak National Monument

13) What option do the parents prefer?
   A Tithe Museum
   B Penny Park
   C Speedy's Fun Fair
   D Seacombe Beach
   E Peak National Monument

14) What would be the children's last choice?
   A Tithe Museum
   B Penny Park
   C Speedy's Fun Fair
   D Seacombe Beach
   E Peak National Monument

15) Which option has the highest rating?
   A Tithe Museum
   B Penny Park
   C Speedy's Fun Fair
   D Seacombe Beach
   E Peak National Monument

A newsagent offers a range of five newspapers. Newspapers B, D and E contain full TV programme listings for the week. Newspapers A and D come with free celebrity magazines that are popular with teenage readers. There is a culture review section in newspaper B each day of the week. Newspaper D is the most expensive option. Newspapers C and D come with a section on residential properties for sale. Newspaper C is the least expensive. Newspapers A and E feature job listings every day of the week; E's are local listings and A's are national job listings. Newspapers A and E also have weekend editions.

Which newspaper would each of the following prefer to choose from this newsagent?

16) A teenager looking nationally for a job who does not have much money to spend on a newspaper.
   A Newspaper A
   B Newspaper B
   C Newspaper C
   D Newspaper D
   E Newspaper E

17) A local resident who wants to look for local job listings on a
weekend.
   A Newspaper A
   B Newspaper B
   C Newspaper C
   D Newspaper D
   E Newspaper E

18) A married couple who want to read a culture section and
also have a full TV guide in the newspaper that they buy.
   A Newspaper A
   B Newspaper B
   C Newspaper C
   D Newspaper D
   E Newspaper E

19) A newcomer to the area who wants to buy the cheapest
newspaper with local houses listed for sale in it.
   A Newspaper A
   B Newspaper B
   C Newspaper C
   D Newspaper D
   E Newspaper E

20) An unemployed builder who wants to use his newspaper to
look for a job as well as having a celebrity magazine to read
afterwards.
   A Newspaper A
   B Newspaper B
   C Newspaper C
   D Newspaper D
   E Newspaper E

The answers to this section are found on pages 125–126.

Armed Forces – Answers

Army – Letter checking

1)	B	1
2)	E	4
3)	A	0
4)	B	1
5)	C	2
6)	C	2
7)	C	2
8)	E	4
9)	D	3
10)	E	4
11)	A	0
12)	E	4
13)	E	4
14)	A	0
15)	A	0
16)	D	3
17)	D	3
18)	C	2
19)	B	1
20)	D	3
21)	D	3
22)	B	1
23)	B	1
24)	B	1
25)	B	1

Army – Reasoning

1)	B	Paul
2)	A	Raj
3)	A	Sally
4)	B	Pauline
5)	B	Gene

6)	A	Siri
7)	B	Sarah
8)	B	Roger
9)	A	Graham
10)	B	Harry
11)	B	Asha
12)	B	Gordon
13)	A	Jack
14)	B	Zack
15)	A	Isaac
16)	B	Shoaib
17)	A	Evelyn
18)	B	Freddy
19)	B	Andy
20)	B	Jason
21)	A	Manuel
22)	A	Gary
23)	A	Raymond
24)	B	Dirk
25)	B	Geoffrey

Army – Odd one out

1)	A	hat
2)	B	arm
3)	C	pull
4)	B	computer
5)	A	fist
6)	A	diamond
7)	B	heavy
8)	B	whisper
9)	B	keeper
10)	C	baby
11)	B	sweat
12)	B	wing
13)	B	name

14)	B	jumper
15)	A	bungalow
16)	C	jeep
17)	A	water
18)	B	enable
19)	B	attack
20)	A	bench
21)	B	event
22)	C	cash
23)	C	gate
24)	B	join
25)	A	take

Navy – Reasoning

1)	B	DRINK
2)	A	WARM
3)	C	HOUSES
4)	A	AMBIGUOUS
5)	C	IMPOSSIBLE
6)	B	DRIVER
7)	D	EASY
8)	B	IRREGULAR
9)	E	WALK
10)	A	NEW
11)	C	UNFAIR
12)	D	ERASE
13)	A	USE
14)	D	SCARCE
15)	E	SHIP
16)	C	COMPARABLE
17)	E	LEISURELY
18)	D	TIME
19)	A	COMPLETE
20)	C	GENEROUS

Navy – Verbal Ability

1)   E   wean
2)   C   hat
3)   A   dilapidated
4)   B   ion
5)   D   house
6)   B   I have not yet eaten my dinner.
7)   D   dam
8)   C   pet
9)   E   thrifty
10)   C   idea
11)   A   vehicle
12)   E   The boy still needs to walk his dog.
13)   E   tong
14)   B   colour
15)   C   outbursts
16)   D   den
17)   D   shop
18)   B   man
19)   A   The shop is only open at the weekend.
20)   B   burn
21)   B   furniture
22)   D   confidence
23)   E   eon
24)   A   flower
25)   E   Tomorrow the weather will improve.
26)   B   sort
27)   C   vegetable
28)   E   food
29)   D   Richard thanked Erica for the birthday present she gave him.
30)   A   age
31)   D   number
32)   D   animated

33)	B	ion
34)	C	profession
35)	A	Brian sold his stamp collection.
36)	D	steal
37)	B	shoe
38)	E	dangerous
39)	C	bed
40)	A	weather
41)	B	Fred bought a cake at the fair.
42)	B	tail
43)	E	metal
44)	E	tactfully
45)	B	nil
46)	B	instrument
47)	D	The teacher was presented with an award by the pupil.
48)	E	fill
49)	A	book
50)	B	studied
51)	E	side
52)	C	fruit
53)	C	My library book is now overdue.
54)	E	tend
55)	D	animal
56)	C	sophisticated
57)	C	Last year we went on holiday to the seaside.
58)	E	tool

RAF – Verbal Reasoning

1)	D	Thriller
2)	B	Nicola
3)	A	Romance and action
4)	C	Hifzu, Carol
5)	E	Can't Tell
6)	D	Mrs Jenkins

7)   B   Mrs Kaur
8)   D   Mrs Jenkins
9)   E   Mr Hays
10) A   Mr Phillips
11) B   Penny Park
12) B   Penny Park
13) A   Tithe Museum
14) E   Peak National Monument
15) E   Peak National Monument
16) A   Newspaper A
17) E   Newspaper E
18) B   Newspaper B
19) C   Newspaper C
20) A   Newspaper A

CHAPTER 8

Qualified Teacher Status (QTS) Literacy Test

Anyone who is attempting to become a teacher – whatever subject they intend to specialise in – must take three computerised tests in literacy, numeracy and ICT. Passing all three of these tests is a prerequisite in England for attaining Qualified Teacher Status. QTS is needed to teach at a maintained school (or a non-maintained school as a qualified teacher). You might be wondering why you need to take a literacy test if you don't plan to become an English teacher. The answer is simple – effective communication, both written and spoken, is absolutely essential to the teaching profession. One way in which candidates' communication skills are assessed is by sitting a literacy test.

How is it taken?

For security and confidentiality reasons you can't take the test from the comfort of your own home. Instead, the test is taken online under supervised test conditions at a testing centre. The three tests can be taken altogether in one sitting or one at a time. There are approximately 50 QTS skills test centres around the country, at locations such as schools, universities and further education colleges, as well as commercial testing centres. Details of how to book these tests and information on what to take along on the testing day can be found on the internet at http://www.tda.gov.uk/skillstests.aspx.

> **brilliant tip**
>
> You will be provided with very specific onscreen instructions before starting each test. Pay close attention to these – especially to how the instructions change between the different sub-tests.

What is the pass mark?

There are 48 available marks on the literacy test – one per question. Depending on which version of the test you take, the pass mark varies a bit – it is lower for a test with slightly harder questions and higher for a test with slightly easier questions. That said, the pass mark for the benchmarked literacy test is 60 per cent – or 29 marks out of the 48 available. Your result will be given to you at the end of the day. Fear not – if you do not pass on your first attempt, the QTS tests can be retaken.

What does it test?

The QTS Literacy Test is designed to assess a trainee teacher's basic foundation in literacy and their ability to apply this within a professional teaching role at a school. The QTS is specifically designed to test verbal reasoning in an educational context. The questions and passages reflect the sort of texts that teachers are likely to encounter at school. This is what's called a highly face valid test.

The 45-minute test is divided into four sub-tests. It starts with a spelling test, followed by three others – punctuation, grammar and comprehension. These last three sub-tests can be completed in any order in the real test. To complete the test you need to be proficient at using a computer keyboard to type in answers. You will also need to scroll down to read long passages of text, and to be able to drag and drop your selected answer into its correct position in the passage.

There follow four practice tests – one for each of the four literacy sub-tests. The practice questions mirror the difficulty and different types of question that you are likely to encounter.

Additional resources

The following website provides additional general information on the test:

http://www.tda.gov.uk/skillstests.aspx

The following website contains some excellent practice materials:

http://www.tda.gov.uk/skillstests/literacy/practicematerials.aspx

The government's directgov website contains useful information on the role, the qualifications required and how to apply, simply search for specific teaching roles at:

http://careersadvice.direct.gov.uk/helpwithyourcareer/jobprofiles

There is some basic guidance on areas such as grammar, spelling and vocabulary at the BBC's skillswise site:

http://www.bbc.co.uk/skillswise

QTS – Spelling

This section of the QTS Literacy Test measures your ability to spell correctly. This is an audio test in which you listen to the questions through headphones. You need to use standard English spellings. This is not a 'spelling bee' in which you would be asked to spell progressively harder words. Instead, the words that you are being tested on are those that many pupils regularly use incorrectly. In other words, these are exactly the mistakes that a teacher needs to be able to recognise and correct!

Instructions

Each question presents you with a sentence. This sentence contains a missing word. Insert the correct missing word from the four options. Although the practice questions that follow have a written format, they are at the same difficulty level as the audio test.

brilliant tips

- Remember to go back and listen to a word again if you have time and are unsure of your answer.
- Memorise the correct spelling of any words you misspell on the practice test.
- Re-learn a few simple spelling rules if you have forgotten them, e.g. i before e except after c. Also, to make a word ending in 'y' a plural add 'ies', e.g. party becomes parties (not partys!).
- Learning how to spell a new word is easier when you say it aloud. Can you work out how to write it based on how it sounds?

Practice questions

1) Thanks to a _____ grant from a benefactor, the school built a new science wing.

| generous |
| generose |
| genarous |
| genereus |

2) The school library offers free _____ to books for all pupils, especially early learners and young readers.

assess
access
acces
acess

3) Pupils in their final year at secondary school undertake a _____ project.

reserch
resarch
recearch
research

4) The _____ summer fair is a highlight of the school year.

annual
anual
annuele
annuelle

5) All potential parents will _____ notification of entry requirements in due course.

reccieve
receive
recieve
reseive

6) New staff must be fully briefed in the fire drill _____.

precedure
preecedure
procedure
proceedere

7) Oakfield School was presented with a certificate for its exemplary _____.

    attendance
    atendence
    atendance
    attendence

8) A full _____ to cooperate with school teachers is one of the things that we expect of our students.

    cometment
    commitment
    comitment
    comittment

9) Our pupils continue to enjoy academic and sporting _____.

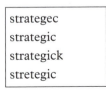

    sucess
    suckcess
    succes
    success

10) The school governors voted _____ to introduce a gifted and talented policy.

    unanimosly
    unanimossly
    unanimosously
    unanimously

11) The Governing Body has considerable input into the _____ direction of the school.

    strategec
    strategic
    strategick
    stretegic

12) St Peter's School encourages _____ in a wide range of after-school activities.

> involvement
> envolvement
> involement
> involvment

13) The school _____ is always available to deal with any parental concerns.

> principal
> principle
> princapal
> principel

14) Our school takes a strong stance when _____ with bullying.

> deeling
> dealaling
> dealing
> delling

15) The new head must tackle the recent rise in disciplinary _____.

> incidents
> incidence
> encidents
> incidences

16) Children in reception learn their numbers and the letters of the _____.

> alphabete
> alphabet
> alphabette
> alferbet

17) The school canteen offers a balanced diet, including a different _____ option each day.

vegetarian
vegatarian
vegeterian
vegetarien

18) A teacher's day involves a great deal of _____ outside of school hours.

preperation
preparation
preparetion
preperetion

19) Children took part in _____ activities during our 'healthy living' week.

physicale
physical
pysikal
phsical

20) It is not possible to _____ a school place for siblings.

garantee
guaranty
guarantee
guarante

21) The academy has a specialist science and maths _____.

coriculum
curiculum
curriculum
curriculem

22) It is more _____ to compare the school's result
with others locally.

relevent
relivent
relevente
relevant

23) The school aims to provide a secure and _____
environment in which to teach and learn.

pleasent
pleshent
pleashent
pleasant

24) The newspaper article was _____ to last year's
results.

refering
referring
reffering
reafering

25) The student body reflects the catchment area's diverse

_____ .

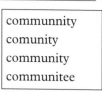

communnity
comunity
community
communitee

26) The college is _____ some new courses this
term.

trailing
trialing
trialling
trailling

27) The school took the _____ measures to lift its rating.

> necessery
> neccessary
> necassary
> necessary

28) Payeton High has the highest _____ record in the borough.

> absense
> absence
> absunse
> absance

29) Final-year pupils are provided with practical _____ advice.

> carear
> carer
> career
> carea

30) Infant pupils _____ transfer to the junior school.

> automaticaly
> automatically
> altermatically
> altermaticaly

31) The Parents' Association acts now as a _____ between the school and the pupils' families.

> liason
> liasion
> liaison
> leason

32) Children   participate   in   a   weekly   dance   and   drama

_____.

> session
> seshion
> sechion
> sesion

33) It   was   discovered   that   the   child's   hearing   was

_____.

> empared
> impared
> impaired
> empaired

34) St Mark's provides children of its parish with an out-standing _____ education

> religisise
> religeus
> religous
> religious

35) The   junior   and   senior   schools   are   housed   in
_____ buildings.

> separate
> seperate
> seperete
> seperite

36) Information _____ is incorporated into every subject area.

> tecknology
> technology
> technologie
> teknology

37) Many students used the evening as an _____ to gain their first experience of adult learning.

> opportunety
> oppertunity
> oportunity
> opportunity

38) The primary school does not allow pupils to bring or to wear _____ to class.

> jewelery
> jewelary
> jewellery
> jewellary

39) In this case the pupil's response was clearly _____.

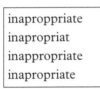

> inaproppriate
> inapropriat
> inappropriate
> inapropriate

40) At the meeting a decision was taken to increase class sizes in order to _____ the higher expected intake of pupils.

> accomadate
> accomodate
> accommodate
> acommodate

The answers to this sectiom are on pages 156–157.

QTS – Punctuation

This section of the QTS Literacy Test measures your ability to apply effective punctuation to set passages. Accurate punctuation is a key element of written communication. Badly punctuated writing is like a road without road markings – it is all too easy for the reader to get lost and confused.

Instructions

You will be presented with a block of text with missing or incorrect punctuation. You need to highlight each punctuation error and also where missing punctuation should be inserted.

This will be done in a computerised format in the actual test. There will be a block of all the possible punctuation marks and the letters of the alphabet on screen. You will drag the correct punctuation from this block to its position in the passage.

Remember that punctuation needs to be consistent. For example, if the passage contains a list with items separated by semicolons except for one item separated by a comma, then you should change the comma to a semicolon. In some instances, punctuation is a matter of personal preference. For example, some people like to use dashes; other people prefer parentheses. If you are unsure look at how the rest of the passage is punctuated. Make sure that whatever corrections you make are consistent with the rest of the passage.

brilliant tip

Do an initial run-through of the text picking up the easiest punctuation errors. Then do a more careful sweep. Do a final check – time permitting – to ensure that you haven't missed anything out. It's impossible to predict where the errors will appear. But it is likely that the errors will be spread out across the entire passage. This means that most sentences will contain at least one error.

Practice questions

Question 1

The creation of new Academies is one of labours flagship policies. According to the newspaper *the new daily gazette,* a four year enquiry has raised some controversial questions. For example will there be enough sponsor's? Where will the teachers come from. Support My Schools an education charity has highlighted the limited range of facilities available and suggests that the academies are not doing enough to serve their local communities

However a recent review conducted by handerson consultancy gives the following evidence in support of academy expansion many outstanding ratings have been given to existing academies several academies are already oversubscribed and their student's gcse exam results have improved. Commenting on the report, Geoffrey Day, headmaster of greve academy, said 'our goal is to provide an excellent education for our communtitys young men and women and this report shows that we are succeeding.

Question 2 – Diplomas

The complicated, diploma programme for educating 14 to 19 year olds aims to fill the gap between Secondary School and higher education. Sounds simple enough, doesn't it. However critic's point to the difficulty of building a shared understanding across those parties involved local employers, schools and fe colleges others have highlighted the lack of commonality between the five, diploma subject areas ranging from: media through to construction/built environment!

Paul murphy, head of FE at springbrook college emphasises, 'We need to provide better practical training for young adults. Lets do this now' For mr Murphy at least this issue takes Priority over achieving a consensus among those delivering the new diplomas. he adds 'When nvqs were introduced they also met with resistance but became a long term success.

The answers to this sectiom are on pages 157–161.

QTS – Grammar

This section of the QTS Literacy Test measures your ability to use good grammar, an essential component of effective written and spoken communication.

Instructions

In the actual test you will need to select the correct phrase or sentence to insert into a short passage. You will be presented with several choices, only one of which is grammatically correct. In the practice questions below, identify which sentence is grammatically correct.

It might appear to contradict previously given advice, but I think it's key to take your time with the grammar test. Carefully read and interpret the sentences – many of the options will be similar, and you need to pay close attention to detail in order to spot the errors. Good grammar requires consistency. So check that the tenses, the pronouns, the case, and the person are consistent throughout the set of statements.

brilliant tip

Listen out for examples of incorrect grammar in your everyday life – they shouldn't be hard to find! Think about what is wrong – and what the correct phrasing should be.

Practice questions

Question 1
A) If the OFSTED inspectors do not see an improvement when they return to the school, the head will have to resign.
B) If the OFSTED inspectors do not see an improvement when they return to the school, the head will have had to resign.

C) If the OFSTED inspectors do not see an improvement when they return to the school, the head would have had to have resigned.

D) If the OFSTED inspectors do not see an improvement when they return to the school, the head would have resigned.

Question 2

A) Child development as a field of study covers all kinds of subject.

B) Child development as a field of study covers all kind of subject.

C) Child development as a field of study covers different kinds of subject.

D) Child development as a field of study covers all kinds of subjects.

Question 3

A) Reading to pre-school-aged children has a positive affect on their literacy.

B) Reading to pre-school-aged children has a positive effect on their literacy.

C) Reading to pre-school-aged children is affective at promoting literacy.

D) Reading to pre-school-aged children will effect their literacy in a positive way.

Question 4

A) Considering how much revision the student did, her exam results could of been better.

B) Considering how much revision the student did, her exam results should of been better.

C) Considering how much revision the student did, her exam results should have been better.

D) Considering how much revision the student did, her exam results must have been better.

Question 5

A) We was prepared for the Christmas concert when the fire alarm went off.

B) We were preparing for the Christmas concert when the fire alarm went off.

C) We was preparing for the Christmas concert when the fire alarm went off.

D) We will be prepared for the Christmas concert when the fire alarm went off.

Question 6

A) When the next academic year starts, there will be many new pupils, each of whom is learnt the school rules.

B) When the next academic year starts, there is many new pupils who are each learning the school rules.

C) When the next academic year starts, there are many new pupils to learn the school rules.

D) When the next academic year starts, there will be many new pupils who will each learn the school rules.

Question 7

A) There are many books that pupils can take out of the library but their not allowed to take them out for more than two weeks at a time.

B) There are many books that pupils can take out of the library but they're not allowed to take them out for more than two weeks at a time.

C) These are the many books that pupils can take out of the library but their not allowed to take them out for more than two weeks at a time.

D) Here there is many books that pupils can take out of the library but they're not allowed to take them out for more than two weeks at a time.

Question 8

A) Me and the teacher looked over the solution to the maths problem.

B) The teacher showed myself how to solve the maths problem.

C) Myself and the teacher looked over the solution to the maths problem.

D) The teacher showed me the solution to the maths problem.

Question 9

A) Children must remember to wear their plimsolls when you have PE classes.

B) Children are forgetting to wear plimsolls when you have PE classes.

C) Children must remember to wear their plimsolls when they have PE classes.

D) Children must not forget to wear your plimsolls to PE classes.

Question 10

A) He and I are presenting a paper at a national teachers' conference next week.

B) Me and him are presenting a paper at a national teachers' conference next week.

C) He and me are presenting a paper at a national teachers' conference next week.

D) Him and myself are presenting a paper at a national teachers' conference next week.

Question 11

A) Peter was the eldest of the two brothers.

B) Peter was the elder of the two brothers.

C) Peter was more older than his brother.

D) Peter was more elder than his brother.

Question 12

A)   Every sort of book is available on how to rear your child.

B)   All sorts of book is available on how to rear your child.

C)   Every sort of book are available on how to rear your child.

D)   Each sort of books are available on how to rear your child.

Question 13

A)   Of all the swimmers on the team this year, Alex is the faster swimmer.

B)   Of all the swimmers on the team this year, Alex is the most fast.

C)   Of all the swimmers on the team this year, Alex is the fastest.

D)   Of all the swimmers on the team this year, Alex is faster.

Question 14

A)   It was the new teacher's stricter regime whom the parents preferred.

B)   It was the new teacher's stricter regime who the parents preferred.

C)   It was the new teacher's stricter regime that the parents preferred.

D)   It was the new teacher's stricter regime with which the parents preferred.

Question 15

A)   After raising enough money at the summer fair, the new computer software was purchased by the PTA.

B)   After raising enough money at the summer fair, the PTA purchased new computer software.

C)   After raising enough money at the summer fair, the money was used by the PTA to purchase new computer software.

D)   After raising enough money at the summer fair, the new computer software was bought by the PTA.

Question 16

A) The teaching assistant told the pupils to use these crayons to decorate their masks.

B) The teaching assistant told the pupils to use them crayons to decorate their masks.

C) The teaching assistant told the pupils to use that crayons to decorate their masks.

D) The teaching assistant told the pupils to use there crayons to decorate their masks.

Question 17

A) Maths and science is his strongest subject, although he also has an aptitude for languages.

B) Maths and science are his strongest subjects, although he also has an aptitude for languages.

C) Maths and science are his strongest subject, although he also has an aptitude for languages.

D) Maths and science is his strongest subjects, although he also has an aptitude for languages.

Question 18

A) The teacher to who the award was given has been promoted to deputy head.

B) The teacher who the award was given to has been promoted to deputy head.

C) The teacher to whom the award was given has been promoted to deputy head.

D) The teacher whom was given the award has been promoted to deputy head.

Question 19

A) The highly critical report stated that a five-year-old had been left to fend for themself at the swimming pool.

B) A five-year-old child had been left to fend for themselves at the swimming pool, according to a highly critical report.

C) The highly critical report stated that a five-year-old child was left to fend for itself at the swimming pool.

D) The highly critical report states that five-year-old children should not be left to fend for themselves at the swimming pool.

The answers to this section are on pages 161–165.

QTS – Comprehension

This section of the QTS Literacy Test measures your ability to fully comprehend passages of text. Your understanding will be tested in many different ways, including:

- Presenting the same information in a different way;
- Identifying the key points;
- Distinguishing between what is portrayed as fact and fiction;
- Inferences;
- Deductions.

There are several different question types that you might encounter in the comprehension test. One question format asks you to identify the particular audience that a passage or extract is aimed at. Go with your instinct. Think about the reading level and tone. Does it sound like school policy to you? Does it read as though it is information for teachers? Is the piece's reading level accessible to pupils?

Another question format asks you to suggest summary headings. Analyse the main point(s) of the paragraph objectively. What key point should be highlighted? Don't be misled by something that's only mentioned once in a single phrase or sentence. It can be helpful, particularly if you are short of time, to focus on the first and last sentences in a paragraph. This is where you are likely to find the topic sentence. In a well-written paragraph, the topic sentence summarises the paragraph's main point.

For each passage you need to consider both the overall meaning and the detail. To assess the bigger picture, ask yourself questions such as: What is the main message? Who is the intended audience? When reflecting on the passage's detail ask yourself: What are the facts? What's the most important information in a passage?

It is not possible to cover the full range of different question types that can be found in the QTS comprehension test. Some of the more common ones are listed below, but don't be alarmed if you are asked to do something different to what's been covered here – there are numerous ways to test reading comprehension.

- summarising the main points that the passage makes;
- evaluating whether statements are supported, contradicted or implied by the information in the passage;
- placing statements based on the passage into set categories;
- putting sentences about a passage describing sequential events into the correct order.

Instructions

Read the extract and then answer the subsequent questions. Don't rush to answer questions without referring back to the passage. Even if you think that you know the answer without looking it's always worth double-checking. First check against the question and then against the passage. You need to be 100 per cent happy with your answer. If it isn't quite what you were looking for then it is probably wrong.

brilliant tip

For more information about reading comprehension tests see Chapter 4.

Practice questions

Passage 1

All children need to master spelling. This is one of the key skills for effective written communication. In order to express themselves and make their ideas understood by others, children must learn to write using correct grammar and spelling. Although the importance of spelling cannot be underestimated, teachers also need to ensure that young pupils do not restrict their vocabulary to those words that they know how to spell correctly.

A more widespread use of successful spelling programmes needs to be encouraged in primary schools. One method that has proven particularly popular is the spelling journal. This records words that are commonly spelt incorrectly and identifies exceptions to rules (for example pluralising words ending in y). Another effective spelling programme is the use of mnemonics. The use of such memory aids can make spelling lessons more enjoyable and engaging. Some primary schools create a spelling log containing words that children use most frequently in their writing. To learn these spellings the child is taught to look at the word, to say it out loud, to cover it up, to try to write it down and then to check that it has been spelt correctly.

For maximum success, parents, as well as teachers, need to ensure that children practise their spelling. Targets can be set, such as personalised lists of frequently misspelt words, and shared with parents. Parents can then supervise revision of these target words as part of their child's homework.

Task A Select the best heading for the passage:

- Spelling test
- How to spell
- Spelling policy
- Mnemonics

Task B Select from the list below those two options that are the closest in meaning to the following phrase as it appears within the passage: Another effective spelling programme is the use of mnemonics.

- Memory aids are an unreliable technique for teaching spelling.
- Memory aids are an unpopular technique for teaching spelling.
- Memory aids are an ineffective technique for teaching spelling.
- Memory aids are a useful technique for teaching spelling.
- Memory aids are a successful technique for teaching spelling.

Task C Select the best sub-heading for the second and third paragraphs:

Second paragraph
- Spelling programmes
- Spelling logs
- Teaching spelling
- Parental involvement

Third paragraph
- Spelling programmes
- Spelling targets
- Teaching spelling
- Parental involvement

Task D A list of seven possible audiences for the text are presented below. Select the two potential audiences that you think would find the passage most relevant:

- parents of primary school children

- pupils
- primary school teachers
- students studying for A-levels
- educational publishers
- school Governors
- secondary school teachers

Passage 2

The new head teacher used a curriculum map to restructure his school's curriculum. The aim was to deliver Key Skills as effectively as possible. Within this overall goal were two specific needs. Firstly, to accommodate the different learning styles of the school's diverse range of pupils. Secondly, but equally as important, to address each child's developmental needs.

Since the adoption of this new plan, the school has demonstrated strength in setting challenging targets at both Key Stage 1 and Key Stage 2. Target setting and pupil attainment are closely monitored. Analysis of the school's results revealed the following: achievement at Key Stage 2 was above the national target, and Key Stage 1 results were above those of comparable local schools. Although its pupils' performance has varied during the period under review, the school has now improved its Key Stage 1 results for three years in a row.

Another target that the school has achieved is a wider application of information and communication technology (ICT) to support the learning process. The previous head teacher had prioritised the application of ICT across the full curriculum, starting with the provision of several new computers in each classroom. The new head has continued this process by establishing a dedicated ICT laboratory and investing in computerised whiteboards for each classroom.

Task A Select the most appropriate sub-heading for the final paragraph:

- ICT implementation
- Key Stage 1 and 2 target setting
- Pupil enrichment programme
- The prioritisation of information and communication technology

Task B Select the sentence that summarises paragraphs one and two most effectively:

Paragraph one

- The school set and met high targets for both Key Stage 1 and Key Stage 2.
- A curriculum map was used to plan and monitor the school targets.
- The new head teacher's planning of two specific Key Skills targets.
- Key skills and curriculum planning took account of individual learning styles and development needs.

Paragraph two

- There were performance differences in Key Stage 1 but not in Key Stage 2 results.
- The school set and met high targets for both Key Stage 1 and Key Stage 2.
- Key skills planning took account of the needs of individual pupils.
- The school closely monitored its Key Stage 1 and Key Stage 2 targets.

Task C Select four phrases from the list below that accurately convey the school's performance (using only the information given in the passage):

- Key Stage 1 results improved for three years consecutively.
- There were no differences in how different pupil cohorts performed.
- Key Stage 1 results were better than those of equivalent schools.
- The national target for Key Stage 2 was below the school's results.
- Key Stage 1 results improved for four years in a row.
- Pupils' results have not always been consistent during the time period under consideration.
- Achievement at Key Stage 1 was above the national target.
- The Key Stage 1 and 2 targets need to be set at a higher level.

Task D Select the two statements below that are closest in meaning to the following phrase within the passage: The previous head teacher had prioritized the application of ICT across the full curriculum.

- ICT had been a priority for the previous head teacher.
- The need for improved access to computer facilities had been prioritised.
- ICT had been made part of the wider curriculum.
- The need for improved access to computer facilities had been recognised in the past.

The answers to this section are on page 165–168.

QTS – Answers

Spelling

1) generous
2) access
3) research
4) annual
5) receive
6) procedure
7) attendance
8) commitment
9) success
10) unanimously
11) strategic
12) involvement
13) principal
14) dealing
15) incidents
16) alphabet
17) vegetarian
18) preparation
19) physical
20) guarantee
21) curriculum
22) relevant
23) pleasant
24) referring
25) community
26) trialling
27) necessary
28) absence
29) career
30) automatically
31) liaison
32) session

33) impaired
34) religious
35) separate
36) technology
37) opportunity
38) jewellery
39) inappropriate
40) accommodate

QTS – Punctuation

Question 1

The creation of new academies is one of Labour's flagship policies. According to the newspaper *The New Daily Gazette,* a four-year enquiry has raised some controversial questions. For example, will there be enough sponsors? Where will the teachers come from? Support My Schools, an education charity, has highlighted the limited range of facilities available and suggests that the academies are not doing enough to serve their local communities.

However, a recent review conducted by Handerson Consultancy gives the following evidence in support of academy expansion: many outstanding ratings have been given to existing academies; several academies are already oversubscribed; and their students' GCSE exam results have improved. Commenting on the report, Geoffrey Day, Headmaster of Greve Academy, said, 'Our goal is to provide an excellent education for our community's young men and women and this report shows that we are succeeding.'

SENTENCE 1 *The creation of new academies is one of Labour's flagship policies.*
The word *Academies* does not require a capital letter since it is a common noun.
Labour is a proper noun and so requires a capital letter. A

possessive apostrophe is also needed since the flagship policies belong to the Labour Party.

SENTENCE 2 *According to the newspaper* The New Daily Gazette, *a four-year enquiry has raised some controversial questions.*
As a newspaper name *The New Daily Gazette* requires capital letters.
Four-year requires a hyphen since it is two separate words being used together to modify *enquiry*.

SENTENCE 3 *For example, will there be enough sponsors?*
A comma is needed after *For example* to indicate a pause.
Sponsors is plural, not possessive, so does not need an apostrophe.

SENTENCE 4 *Where will the teachers come from?*
A question mark is needed at the end of the sentence.

SENTENCE 5 *Support My Schools, an education charity, has highlighted the limited range of facilities available and suggests that the academies are not doing enough to serve their local communities.*
Commas are needed around the embedded clause *an education charity*.
A full stop is needed to mark the end of the sentence.

SENTENCE 6 *However, a recent review conducted by Handerson Consultancy gives the following evidence in support of academy expansion: many outstanding ratings have been given to existing academies; several academies are already oversubscribed; and their students' GCSE exam results have improved.*
The sentence opener *However* is followed by a comma.
Handerson Consultancy is a proper noun and so requires capital letters.
A colon is needed before the list of supporting evidence. The items that appear as supporting evidence need to be separated by a semicolon.
Students' is a plural possessive – the exam results belong to all the students, not just one, so the apostrophe goes after the s.

GCSE is an acronym (General Certificate of Secondary Education) so needs capital letters.

SENTENCE 7 *Commenting on the report, Geoffrey Day, Headmaster of Greve Academy, said, 'Our goal is to provide an excellent education for our community's young men and women and this report shows that we are succeeding.'*
Headmaster is a title so requires a capital letter.
Greve Academy is a proper noun so needs capital letters.
A comma is needed before the quotation begins.
A capital letter is needed at the beginning of the quotation.
An apostrophe is needed for *community's* as it is possessive.
A quotation mark is needed after the full stop to mark the end of the quote.

Question 2
The complicated diploma programme for educating 14- to 19-year-olds aims to fill the gap between secondary school and higher education. Sounds simple enough, doesn't it? However, critics point to the difficulty of building a shared understanding across those parties involved: local employers, schools and FE colleges. Others have highlighted the lack of commonality between the five diploma subject areas ranging from media through to construction/built environment.

Paul Murphy, Head of FE at Springbrook College emphasises, 'We need to provide better practical training for young adults. Let's do this now.' For Mr Murphy at least, this issue takes priority over achieving a consensus among those delivering the new diplomas. He adds, 'When NVQs were introduced they also met with resistance but became a long-term success.'

SENTENCE 1 *The complicated diploma programme for educating 14- to 19-year-olds aims to fill the gap between secondary school and higher education.*
The comma between *complicated* and *diploma* is unnecessary as no pause is needed.

Hyphens are needed for 14- to 19-year-olds because the words are being used as a compound noun.

Also *secondary school* does not require capital letters since it is a common noun.

SENTENCE 2 *Sounds simple enough, doesn't it?*
The question *Sounds simple enough, doesn't it?* needs a question mark at the end.

SENTENCE 3 *However, critics point to the difficulty of building a shared understanding across those parties involved: local employers, schools and FE colleges.*
The sentence adverb *However* should be followed by a comma.
The plural noun *critics* does not require a possessive apostrophe.
A colon should be used to introduce the listing of local parties involved.
FE is written with capital letters as it is an acronym.
A full stop is needed at the end of the sentence.

SENTENCE 4 *Others have highlighted the lack of commonality between the five diploma subject areas ranging from media through to construction/built environment.*
The start of the sentence requires a capital letter.
The comma needs to be removed between the words *five* and *diploma* as no pause is needed.
No colon is needed after *ranging from.*
The sentence needs a full stop rather than an exclamation mark at the end.

SENTENCE 5 *Paul Murphy, Head of FE at Springbrook College emphasises, 'We need to provide better practical training for young adults. Let's do this now.'*
Murphy is a surname and a proper noun, hence it starts with a capital letter.
Head requires a capital letter as it is a title.
Springbrook College is a proper noun and so needs to start with capital letters.

An apostrophe is required in *Let's* because it is a contraction of *let* and *us*.

A full stop is needed at the end of the quotation.

SENTENCE 6 *For Mr Murphy at least, this issue takes priority over achieving a consensus among those delivering the new diplomas.*

The title *Mr* requires a capital letter.

A comma after *at least* indicates a pause.

The word *priority* does not require a capital letter.

SENTENCE 7 *He adds, 'When NVQs were introduced they also met with resistance but became a long-term success.'*

He needs a capital letter as it is the start of a sentence.

A comma is required before the quotation begins.

The acronym *NVQ* has capital letters (National Vocational Qualification).

Long-term is hyphenated because it is modifying the noun *success*.

Quotation marks are required at the end of the sentence.

QTS – Grammar

Question 1

A)   If the OFSTED inspectors do not see an improvement when they return to the school, the head will have to resign.

The use of the future tense needs to be consistent throughout the sentence. Option A, which states *the head will have to resign*, is the only sentence that matches this phrase correctly with the future need to see an improvement.

Question 2

D)   Child development as a field of study covers all kinds of subjects.

In the sentence for Question 2 the plural word *kinds* needs to agree with the plural word *subjects*.

Question 3

B)   *Reading to pre-school-aged children has a positive effect on their literacy.*

The words *effect* and *affect* are commonly misused. It is important for you to remember that effect is a noun, whereas affect is a verb. It this case option B is the correct answer since it incorporates the word effect as a noun.

Question 4

C)   *Considering how much revision the student did, her exam results should have been better.*

Modal verbs (e.g. might, should) must be followed by *have*, rather than of. Thus option C is the correct answer because the word *should* is followed by *have*.

Question 5

B)   *We were preparing for the Christmas concert when the fire alarm went off.*

The plural pronoun *we* must be followed by the plural form of the verb in order for the sentence to agree. Sentence B is the only option where these match.

Question 6

D)   *When the next academic year starts, there will be many new pupils who will each learn the school rules.*

This is an example of three of the options (A, B and C) using inconsistent tenses following the use of the future tense in the first phrase of the sentence. Whereas option D uses the appropriate form of the future tense throughout the sentence.

Question 7

B)   *There are many books that pupils can take out of the library but they're not allowed to take them out for more than two weeks at a time.*

They're/their/there are very commonly misused. *They're* is correct here because it is a contraction of *they are*.

Question 8

D)   The teacher showed me the solution to the maths problem.

The pronoun *me* is correct when it is the object of the sentence, as in option D. However *me* can't be used as the subject of a sentence – which is why 'Me and the teacher looked over . . .' is incorrect.

Question 9

C)   Children must remember to wear their plimsolls when they have PE classes.

Children is in the third person, so the correct grammar is for the possessive pronoun – i.e. *their* – to also be in the third person.

Question 10

A)   He and I are presenting a paper at a national teachers' conference next week.

He and *I* are the subjects of the sentence, so the correct grammar in this case is to use *I* as the correct form of the pronoun. This is only found in option A.

Question 11

B)   Peter was the elder of the two brothers.

The comparative form of a word (*elder, wiser, taller*) is used when only two examples are being compared.

Question 12

A)   Every sort of book is available on how to rear your child.

This is the only sentence where the determiner (*every*), the singular subject (*sort*) and singular verb (*is*) agree. The other three options include other determiners (*all, each*) that are inconsistent with either their subject (*sort, sorts*) or their verb (*is, are*).

Question 13

C)   Of all the swimmers on the team this year, Alex is the fastest.

The superlative form of a word (i.e. *fastest, biggest, oldest*) is used when three or more examples are being compared. In this case *all the swimmers* requires the superlative *fastest*.

Question 14

C)   It was the new teacher's stricter regime that the parents preferred.
Option C is the only sentence containing the correct use of grammar. It uses the correct relative pronoun (i.e. *that*) when referring to what the parents preferred. The words *whom* and *who* are not used for objects (i.e. *the stricter regime*) – only for referring to specific people.

Question 15

B)   After raising enough money at the summer fair, the PTA purchased new computer software.
This is the only grammatically correct sentence, as all the other options feature dangling participles – where the participle phrase that begins the sentence does not modify when the new phrase begins. It was the PTA that raised the money at the summer fair, not the new computer software!

Question 16

A)   The teaching assistant told the pupils to use these crayons to decorate their masks.
The answer is the only sentence in which the correct determiner is used – i.e. *these crayons*.

Question 17

B)   Maths and science are his strongest subjects, although he also has an aptitude for languages.
The subject of the sentence is plural – maths *and* science – so the verb needs to be plural (*are*, instead of *is*).

Question 18

C)   The teacher to whom the award was given has been promoted to deputy head.

A handy rule for deciding when to use *who* or *whom* is to substitute *he* or *him* into the sentence. *He* becomes *who*; *Him* becomes *whom*.

For example: The award was given to him.

Thus, the teacher *to whom* the award was given.

Question 19

D)   The highly critical report states that five-year-old children should not be left to fend for themselves at the swimming pool.

In the correct sentence, the plural noun *children* agrees with the plural pronoun *themselves*. In the other sentences the singular child does not agree with the plural *themselves*.

QTS – Comprehension

Passage 1 – *Task A*

Spelling policy

The other options are relevant to particular parts of the passage. However, *Spelling policy* is the best heading since the entire passage is on this subject. Spelling policy summarises the content of the passage.

Passage 1 – *Task B*

- *Memory aids are a useful technique for teaching spelling.*

- *Memory aids are a successful technique for teaching spelling.*

The words *useful* and *successful* are synonyms for the word 'effective' – thus these are the two correct answers.

Passage 1 – *Task C*

Second paragraph – *Spelling programmes*

Third paragraph – *Parental involvement*

The other options are less effective summaries of the second and third paragraphs. *Spelling log* is just one of the subjects discussed in the second paragraph. The paragraph as a whole concerns *spelling programmes*. The importance of *parental involvement* is clearly highlighted in the third paragraph. While *teaching spelling* is also relevant the key subject described within the third paragraph is *parental involvement*.

Passage 1 – *Task D*

- *Primary school teachers*
- *Parents of primary school children*

The passage focuses on spelling and how both teachers and parents can develop spelling policies. The phrase *primary school teachers* and the words *teachers* and *parents* come up several times. That's a good sign of who the intended audience is.

Passage 2 – *Task A*

> *The prioritisation of information and communication technology*

This is the most appropriate sub-heading for the final paragraph. The other options do not capture the content of the final paragraph as effectively. The final line of the paragraph is concerned with *ICT* implementation. However the *whole* paragraph concerns the school's ICT target and how the previous head teacher prioritised this, including ICT implementation using *a dedicated ICT laboratory and investing in computerised whiteboards for each classroom.*

Passage 2 – *Task B*

Paragraph one

> *Key skills and curriculum planning took account of individual learning styles and development needs.*

This is an effective summary of the first paragraph. Consider the specific points that each part of the paragraph is making, as follows: *the aim was to deliver Key Skills . . . accommodate the different learning styles . . . to address each child's developmental needs.*

Paragraph two

> *The school set and met high targets for both Key Stage 1 and Key Stage 2.*

This is an effective summary of the second paragraph, which starts by explaining that its main subject is about target setting and then builds on this point by specifying how the school has met such targets. As follows: ... *the school has demonstrated strength in setting challenging targets at both Key Stage 1 and Key Stage 2 ... achievement at Key Stage 2 was above the national target, and Key Stage 1 results were above those of comparable local schools.*

Passage 2 – *Task C*

- *Key Stage 1 results improved for three years consecutively.*
- *Key Stage 1 results were better than those of equivalent schools.*
- *The national target for Key Stage 2 was below the school's results.*
- *Pupils' results have not always been consistent during the time period under consideration.*

The second half of the passage refers to several targets which the school has achieved. To answer the question these need to be picked apart and then 'tested' to see if they match any of the statements in the question. Three of the four correct four statements are found in the following parts of the passage: ... *achievement at Key Stage 2 was above the national target, and Key Stage 1 results were above those of comparable local schools ... the school has now improved its Key Stage 1 results for three years in a row.* The fourth, *Pupils' results have not always been consistent during the time period under consideration,* is slightly trickier but does follow from this part of the passage: *Although its pupils' performance has varied during the period under review ...*

Another target that the school has achieved is a wider application of information and communication technology (ICT) to support the learning process. The previous head teacher had prioritised the application of ICT across the full curriculum, starting with the provision of several new computers in each classroom. The new head has continued this process by establishing a dedicated ICT laboratory and investing in computerised whiteboards for each classroom.

Passage 2 – *Task D*

- *ICT had been a priority for the previous head teacher.*
- *ICT had been made part of the wider curriculum.*

CHAPTER 9

UKCAT

British medical and dental schools are highly selective. Each year, an abundance of highly qualified candidates compete for a limited number of places on courses. This is why applicants to most British medical and dental schools will need to take the UKCAT. The test enables universities to select the most suitable candidates from a large pool of talented applicants. Rather than focusing on academic achievements, the UKCAT tests the general mental abilities – such as verbal reasoning – needed to be a successful health care professional.

How is it taken?

The UKCAT Consortium of Medical and Dental Schools and Pearson VUE run the UKCAT test process. You attend one of Pearson VUE's testing centres to take five multiple choice sub-tests: Verbal reasoning; Quantitative reasoning; Abstract reasoning; Decision analysis; and Non-cognitive analysis. There are individual test instructions and separate timed sessions for each sub-test. The total testing time is two hours. Those candidates with special educational needs sit the UKCATSEN version.

Additional resources

The Pearson VUE Website (www.pearsonvue.co.uk) contains a lot of useful information on the UKCAT tests including a case study and details on how the testing process is managed. http://www.pearsonvue.co.uk/OurClients/Pages/UKCAT.aspx

The official UKCAT website also provides further introductory information: www.ukcat.ac.uk.

It also has:

● further practice questions (www.ukcat.ac.uk/pages/details.aspx?page=practice Questions);

● answer keys for these practice questions;

● hints and tips;

● an online testing demo to familiarise you with the test format;

● a test centre tour to familiarise you with a typical Pearson Professional Centre.

It's always worth checking the official UKCAT website, to stay informed of any format changes. UKCAT was most recently updated in 2009 and the passage length has been increased.

How is it used?

The universities in the UKCAT Consortium use the test results in differing ways. Some of the medical and dental schools apply a cut-off – applicants scoring below a certain level will not progress. Other schools do not apply a cut-off score but consider the results alongside other criteria, such as academic performance, a personal statement and an interview. You will need to contact the relevant schools for details of their admissions policies.

Instructions

For the UKCAT verbal reasoning test, you will have one minute for reading the test instructions, followed by 21 minutes to answer 44 questions. You will be presented with 11 passages, each followed by four statements. Read each passage and decide whether each statement is TRUE, FALSE or whether you CAN'T TELL.

Your answer must be based only on the information given in the passage. Do not consider your own knowledge when answering the questions. The passages will be extracted from a wide range of sources. As far as you are concerned, these extracts are all based on fact. Do not be misled if the extract presents someone's opinion or different sides of an argument.

Manage your time carefully. The average length of time for answering each question is just under 30 seconds. Of course you also need to allow for the time you will spend reading and interpreting the passages. Your best timekeeping strategy might be to wait until half the test time has passed (11 minutes) and then check that you are at least halfway through the questions. If yes, then maintain a steady pace. If no, then speed up!

For more advice about this sort of test format, see Chapter 4.

brilliant tip

Make sure you understand the three answer options:

- TRUE means the statement is true or follows logically from the information given in the passage.
- FALSE means the statement is false – based only on the information given in the passage.
- CAN'T TELL means you cannot say whether it is true or false because there is insufficient information given in the passage.

Do you understand the difference? It is incredibly easy for people to confuse these answer options. Remember that your answers are interpreting what was said in the passage. A TRUE answer can mean that the statement itself can be read in the passage OR that the statement follows on logically from the passage.

Practice questions

The UKCAT format has four questions associated with each passage of text. Here each passage has five related questions so that you get additional practice. There are 14 passages and 70 questions in total – that's almost double the length of the UKCAT verbal reasoning test, so I'd recommend splitting these questions up into two practice sessions.

The Large Hadron Collider (LHC), located underneath the border of France and Switzerland, is one of the biggest pieces of machinery in the world. Its construction involved 9,000 magnets, and over 10,000 tons of nitrogen are used for its cooling processes. Scientists and engineers have spent £4.5 billion on building an underground track at CERN, the world's largest particle physics laboratory. This enormous scientific instrument will collect a huge amount of data, but only a small percentage of what is recorded will be useful. When proton atoms – travelling almost at the speed of light – collide inside the LHC, theoretical physicists expect new forces and particles to be produced. It may even be possible to study black holes using this experiment.

1) Protons travel around the LHC at the speed of light.

   True/False/Can't Tell

2) The cost of the LHC's track was over £4.5 billion.

   True/False/Can't Tell

3) The LHC is the largest experiment ever conducted in the world.

   True/False/Can't Tell

4) The LHC was designed to study black holes.

   True/False/Can't Tell

5) The LHC uses over 10,000 tons of oxygen for its cooling processes.

   True/False/Can't Tell

Large areas of land are needed for growing plants that will be distilled into biofuels. Producing biofuels from agricultural commodities has forced up the price of food. This is just one of the negative impacts that increased biofuel production has had on food security. In August, food scientist Sharon de Cruz demanded an immediate financial review of the current system of subsidies. Her argument is that there are more cost-efficient ways of supporting biofuels. For example, studies have indicated that genetically modifying crops will improve their suitability for producing biofuels.

6)   Sharon de Cruz made a scientific recommendation based on environmental concerns.

True/False/Can't Tell

7)   Genetically modified crops produce biofuels more efficiently.

True/False/Can't Tell

8)   Too much land is required to produce biofuels.

True/False/Can't Tell

9)   Food security is improved by the increased use of biofuels.

True/False/Can't Tell

10) Subsidies represent one way of supporting biofuel production.

True/False/Can't Tell

The frequency of MRSA being given as the cause of death on death certificates has been increasing significantly for several years. MRSA is an infection-causing bacterium that has developed a resistance to penicillin and many other antibiotics. MRSA infections represent a particular danger for hospital patients with weakened immune systems or open wounds.

Scientific trials are testing whether MRSA develops resistance after exposure to new drugs. A research breakthrough would herald a cure for the MRSA threat.

11) MRSA is resistant to all antibiotics.

True/False/Can't Tell

12) MRSA-related deaths are now more common.

True/False/Can't Tell

13) Further research is being conducted to study MRSA.

True/False/Can't Tell

14) Penicillin is an effective treatment for MRSA.

True/False/Can't Tell

15) MRSA can prove fatal.

True/False/Can't Tell

There are now several million cars in the UK using satellite navigation systems (satnav systems). These increasingly popular satnav systems mean that motorists no longer have to read maps while they are driving. There are two other major advantages: reduced journey time and reduced mileage (and thus fuel consumption) on unfamiliar routes. System improvements have made these devices much more accurate than earlier models, and today's designs are easier to use and have fewer distracting features. Although some safety surveys highlight the dangers of operating dashboard devices while driving, research conducted by one satnav manufacturer showed that nearly 70 per cent of drivers felt calmer and more focused on the road when using a satnav system.

16) Most drivers feel calmer when using a satnav system.

True/False/Can't Tell

17) Controversy remains about the effects that satnav systems have on driver concentration.

True/False/Can't Tell

18) Satellite navigation systems are useful for those people who can't read maps.

True/False/Can't Tell

19) The passage suggests that a satnav system can make navigation more efficient.

True/False/Can't Tell

20) Early satnav systems were less accurate than modern ones.

True/False/Can't Tell

Peru's Machu Picchu has been a popular tourist destination since it was discovered in 1911. These mountain-top ruins have become one of the most famous symbols of the Incan empire. The difficult terrain surrounding Machu Picchu meant that Spanish conquistadors never discovered the city. It has been theorised, given the virtual inaccessibility of the site, that it was built for religious – rather than economic or military – reasons. This UNESCO world heritage site's 200 buildings include many temples and houses. The construction of these buildings relied upon cutting many perfectly fitting granite blocks without the use of mortar.

21) Machu Picchu served as a religious centre.

True/False/Can't Tell

22) Machu Picchu is a ruined city in Peru.

True/False/Can't Tell

23) Machu Picchu was built in 1911.

True/False/Can't Tell

24) Its valley location protected Machu Picchu from the Spanish conquistadors.

True/False/Can't Tell

25) Skilled stonemasons were involved in Machu Picchu's construction.

True/False/Can't Tell

Over the last ten years the reach and the sophistication of international supply chains has increased. The three main factors influencing global supply chain design are manufacturing operations, distribution and transportation. These logistic networks connect the supplier's base to its end customer goods and services. There are always several companies seeking to maximise their own profits in any single global supply chain. But it is in the interest of each company in the chain to deal with the others fairly, as their mutual success depends on every link in the chain operating efficiently. Failure can also be shared. A supplier experiencing financial difficulties can soon pass its credit problems to other companies – even to more profitable organisations – along the lines of their interconnected supply chain. There are practical measures for avoiding such contagion from defaulting suppliers or manufacturers. One such safety net involves building a network of multiple suppliers, multiple production facilities and multiple storage facilities – though this, of course, is not always possible for smaller companies.

26) Every company in a supply chain should try to make the maximum profit.

True/False/Can't Tell

27) Manufacturing companies who default can spread their credit problems throughout the supply system.

True/False / Can't Tell

28) International supply chains are planned around only three considerations.

True/False/Can't Tell

29) The most sophisticated supply chains have a global reach.

True/False/Can't Tell

30) There is an indiscriminate impact throughout a supply chain if a supplier is experiencing credit difficulties.

True/False/Can't Tell

Digital broadcasting heralds a new paradigm in television broadcasting. This sophisticated broadcasting technology allows broadcasters to offer television with multiple broadcasting choices and interactive capabilities and high-quality sound and image. However, digital broadcasting should not be confused with High-Definition Television, which offers the very best audio and picture clarity. Analogue television may soon become obsolete in the UK. The USA has already made the transition from analogue to digital broadcasting. There, television stations have stopped broadcasting along analogue channels, and any viewers with analogue television sets must use special set-top conversion boxes in order to view programmes. As well as benefiting viewers with superior entertainment options, the switch to digital broadcasting frees up part of the valuable broadcasting spectrum that can then be used for public and emergency services.

31) Digital television offers the best audio and visual quality.

True/False/Can't Tell

32) In the USA, analogue televisions can no longer be used.

True/False/Can't Tell

33) The switch to digital broadcasting benefits the emergency services.

   True/False/Can't Tell

34) The UK will soon convert from analogue to digital broadcasting.

   True/False/Can't Tell

35) A set-top box is necessary in order to access digital broadcasts.

   True/False/Can't Tell

Wildlife expert Dr Boyle spoke at this year's Wildlife Conservation Conference about the lack of a strategy to prevent the imminent extinction of a number of primate species across Asia. Her talk focused on the dangers of hunters and the clearing of tropical rainforests across the continent. Several species of Asian monkey, some only recently discovered, are facing these dual threats to their natural habitats. Dr Boyle differentiated the most at-risk primates as critically endangered, but the talk stressed that other species were also living under constant threat. Dr Boyle's scientific paper presented compelling evidence of the need to halt deforestation, but in some developing Asian economies, where wood is collected for fuel and for sale and land is cleared for farming, human interests currently take precedence over the fate of the region's lower-order primates.

36) One of the attendees of this year's Wildlife Conservation Conference was called Dr Boyle.

   True/False/Can't Tell

37) The passage gives three reasons for the destruction of tropical rainforests.

   True/False/Can't Tell

38) All Asian primates are threatened by extinction.

True/False/Can't Tell

39) Asian monkeys are the most at risk.

True/False/Can't Tell

40) Several types of Asian monkey live in the tropical rain-forests.

True/False/Can't Tell

Critics of modern quasi-non-governmental organisations point to their remoteness, lack of accountability and the difficulty of managing such bureaucratic organisations. Quangos, which operate at arm's length from the government, are often viewed by the public as inefficient and ineffective, spending more time talking about their goals than actually achieving them. Controversial though they may be, there is evidence of a rise in the number of quangos in the UK, though many of these state-run organisations use alternative names such as executive agency, board, council or commission. A recent report that the UK's quangos spent over £1 billion last year on public relations and communications is not likely to improve these organisations' popularity with taxpayers.

41) Modern quangos are entirely independent of government.

True/False/Can't Tell

42) Quango is another way of referring to a quasi-non-governmental organisation.

True/False/Can't Tell

43) The public perceive quangos as inefficient because of their marketing spend.

True/False/Can't Tell

44) The passage suggests that quangos are bureaucratic.

True/False/Can't Tell

45) The terms executive agency and quango are interchangeable.

True/False/Can't Tell

Last month the market research company Du Balle Inc. reported that the organic food sector grew over the past year, but not at the same rate as the previous five years in which the market grew fivefold. An oft-asked question about organic food is – why does it cost so much more? The simple answer is that organically grown products cost more to farm than their conventionally produced counterparts. Higher production costs due to methods such as crop rotation, hand-weeding (rather than pesticides) and the use of animal manure (instead of chemical fertilizers) result in higher costs to the consumer. Sceptics claim that organic foods are no healthier than non-organic foods. But proponents of organic farming counter that organically produced foods contain fewer contaminants – and that these health benefits more than justify the price differential. A spokeswoman from the Organic Farming Association said, 'Organic farming is about sustainability – and this means economic sustainability for struggling farmers, as well as sustainable food production.'

46) Growth in the organic food market is slowing.

True/False/Can't Tell

47) Using animal manure costs more than chemical fertilizers.

True/False/Can't Tell

48) Organically grown food is healthier.

True/False/Can't Tell

49) Organically grown food contains no pesticides and contaminants.

True/False/Can't Tell

50) Organic farms are profitable.

True/False/Can't Tell

The Arctic region around the North Pole lacks specific land boundaries and has alternative definitions, such as its distinctive ecology. The Arctic region's ecosystem is comprised of many species of plant, bird, fish and mammal, including polar bears. There is life above, below and even within this huge ocean of ice. But the natural habitat of these Arctic animals is being threatened by the effects of global warming. Typically the North Pole's ice cap diminishes in summer and then replenishes itself in the winter months. However, scientists speculate that warmer oceans are causing a dramatic thinning of the Arctic's ice during winter that has resulted in ice-free gaps of ocean in the summer. Some experts predict that the entire ice cap will have disappeared by the end of this century.

51) Marine mammals are the only things living in the Arctic.

True/False/Can't Tell

52) The Arctic's seasonal pattern is to reduce in size during the winter months.

True/False/Can't Tell

53) Higher seawater temperatures are making the Arctic melt.

True/False/Can't Tell

54) The Arctic has fixed geographic borders.

True/False/Can't Tell

55) All of the Arctic's ice disappears in the summer.

True/False/Can't Tell

Ethical labels are now widely used on products, such as coffee, to show that the goods in question have been produced in a worker-friendly manner. A ban on child workers is one labour practice to which ethically labelled suppliers must strictly adhere. Despite increased public awareness, many UK retail stores may still be selling products produced by foreign workers paid extremely low wages. Although working conditions have improved in some companies as a result of labelling, sweatshop wages and a lack of union representation remain prevalent in other suppliers from developing countries. There is also a danger that, where ethical codes of practice have been implemented, the supply workers themselves are inadvertently punished with lower pay.

56) Developing countries restrict union representation.

True/False/Can't Tell

57) The use of ethical labelling has not improved working conditions.

True/False/Can't Tell

58) Ethical labelling as an industry is in decline.

True/False/Can't Tell

59) The implemention of ethical codes of practice never backfires on workers.

True/False/Can't Tell

60) The passage suggests that using ethical labels on products can have both a beneficial and a detrimental effect.

True/False/Can't Tell

The UK has a target of cutting its carbon emissions by using renewable sources to generate a third of its electricity by 2020. One option is to invest heavily in building thousands of wind farms around the country. But a key technological issue that remains to be solved is how to efficiently store wind-powered electricity so as to ensure the regularity of supply that is needed by consumers. Other solutions for cutting carbon emissions are to increase the amount of the electricity supplied by nuclear power or to build more coal-fired power stations equipped with carbon capture technology. The carbon capture technology reduces greenhouse gas emissions by capturing and storing carbon dioxide.

61) Wind-powered electricity does not need to be stored before being distributed to consumers.

   True/False/Can't Tell

62) The passage suggests that carbon capture technology reduces carbon dioxide emissions from coal-fired power stations.

   True/False/Can't Tell

63) The UK is on track to meet its 2020 target.

   True/False/Can't Tell

64) Wind farms are a renewable source of energy.

   True/False/Can't Tell

65) The passage considers nuclear power to be a renewable source of energy.

   True/False/Can't Tell

There are several thousand patients waiting for organ transplants in the UK. This urgent need has led to a government review of how best to increase organ donation rates. The introduction of presumed consent – as found in other European countries – has now been put forward as a possible solution. Such a drastic and controversial change, whereby donating organs would become the default option, would require a new legal framework. Among many other proposals, the government's review recommended establishing the following: locally adapted national policies for organ donation; a best practice framework; and a national organisation to coordinate transplants.

66) Presumed consent means that donating your bodily organs is the default option.

True/False/Can't Tell

67) More coordinators are being recruited to organise organ transplants.

True/False/Can't Tell

68) The number of patients waiting for transplants led to the government's review of the current situation.

True/False/Can't Tell

69) One recommendation was to introduce a standard national policy for all hospitals.

True/False/Can't Tell

70) Although it had widespread support, presumed consent was not part of the government's recommendations.

True/False/Can't Tell

UKCAT – Answers

Question	Answer
1	FALSE
2	FALSE
3	CAN'T TELL
4	FALSE
5	FALSE
6	FALSE
7	TRUE
8	CAN'T TELL
9	FALSE
10	TRUE
11	FALSE
12	TRUE
13	TRUE
14	FALSE
15	TRUE
16	TRUE
17	TRUE
18	TRUE
19	TRUE
20	TRUE
21	CAN'T TELL
22	TRUE
23	FALSE
24	FALSE
25	TRUE
26	FALSE
27	TRUE
28	FALSE
29	CAN'T TELL
30	TRUE
31	FALSE
32	FALSE
33	TRUE

34	CAN'T TELL
35	FALSE
36	TRUE
37	TRUE
38	FALSE
39	CAN'T TELL
40	TRUE
41	FALSE
42	TRUE
43	FALSE
44	TRUE
45	TRUE
46	TRUE
47	TRUE
48	CAN'T TELL
49	FALSE
50	CAN'T TELL
51	FALSE
52	FALSE
53	CAN'T TELL
54	FALSE
55	FALSE
56	CAN'T TELL
57	FALSE
58	FALSE
59	FALSE
60	TRUE
61	TRUE
62	TRUE
63	CAN'T TELL
64	TRUE
65	TRUE
66	TRUE
67	CAN'T TELL
68	TRUE

69	FALSE
70	FALSE

UKCAT – Answer explanations

The Large Hadron Collider (LHC), located underneath the border of France and Switzerland, is one of the biggest pieces of machinery in the world. Its construction involved 9,000 magnets, and over 10,000 tons of nitrogen is used for its cooling processes. Scientists and engineers have spent £4.5 billion on building an underground track at CERN, the world's largest particle physics laboratory. This enormous scientific instrument will collect a huge amount of data, but only a small percentage of what is recorded will be useful. When proton atoms – travelling almost at the speed of light – collide inside the LHC, theoretical physicists expect new forces and particles to be produced. It may even be possible to study black holes using this experiment.

1) Protons travel around the LHC at *the speed of light*
   The correct answer is FALSE because the specific section of the passage states *almost at light speed*.

2) The cost of the LHC's track was over £4.5 billion.
   The correct answer is FALSE because the passage states that the exact cost was £4.5 billion.

3) The LHC is the largest experiment ever conducted in the world.
   The correct answer is CAN'T TELL. The last sentence in the passage refers to the LHC as an experiment. The passage also states that the LHC *is one of the biggest pieces of machinery in the world*. There is no additional evidence in the passage from which to draw the conclusion that the LHC must be *the largest experiment ever conducted in the world*.

4) The LHC was designed to study black holes.
   The correct answer is FALSE because the passage states that it may even be possible to study black holes using this

experiment, however this was not the reason why the LHC was designed.

5) The LHC uses over 10,000 tons of oxygen for its cooling processes.

   The correct answer is FALSE because the passage states that *over 10,000 tons of nitrogen are used for its cooling processes.*

Large areas of land are needed for growing plants that will be distilled into biofuels. Producing biofuels from agricultural commodities has forced up the price of food. This is just one of the negative impacts that increased biofuel production has had on food security. In August, food scientist Sharon de Cruz demanded an immediate financial review of the current system of subsidies. Her argument is that there are more cost-efficient ways of supporting biofuels. For example, studies have indicated that genetically modifying crops will improve their suitability for producing biofuels.

6) Sharon de Cruz made a scientific recommendation based on environmental concerns.

   The correct answer is FALSE because the passage states: *In August, food scientist Sharon de Cruz demanded an immediate financial review of the current system of subsidies.* Sharon is indeed a scientist but her recommendation is based on financial reasons rather than environmental concerns.

7) Genetically modified crops produce biofuels more efficiently.

   The correct answer is TRUE because the passage states *studies have indicated that genetically modifying crops will improve their suitability for producing biofuels.*

8) Too much land is required to produce biofuels.

   The correct answer is CAN'T TELL because the passage states *Large areas of land are needed for growing plants that will be distilled into biofuels.* However there is no judgement or evidence provided within the passage that too much land is needed to produce biofuels.

9) Food security is improved by the increased use of biofuels.
The correct answer is FALSE. There is mention of food security as an issue, as follows: producing *biofuels from agricultural commodities has forced up the price of food. This is just one of the negative impacts that increased biofuel production has had on food security.* The passage considers there to be a negative impact, rather than improved food security.

10) Subsidies represent one way of supporting biofuel production.
The correct answer is TRUE. The relevant parts of the passage are as follows: *In August, food scientist Sharon de Cruz demanded an immediate financial review of the current system of subsidies. Her argument is that there are more cost-efficient ways of supporting biofuels.* In other words one way of supporting biofuels is by subsidy.

The frequency of MRSA being given as the cause of death on death certificates has been increasing significantly for several years. MRSA is an infection-causing bacterium that has developed a resistance to penicillin and many other antibiotics. MRSA infections represent a particular danger for hospital patients with weakened immune systems or open wounds. Scientific trials are testing whether MRSA develops resistance after exposure to new drugs. A research breakthrough would herald a cure for the MRSA threat.

11) MRSA is resistant to all antibiotics.
The correct answer is FALSE. The passage does not say that MRSA is resistant to *all* antibiotics, only *to penicillin and many other antibiotics.*

12) MRSA-related deaths are now more common.
The correct answer is TRUE because the passage states that *the frequency of MRSA being given as the cause of death on*

*death certificates has been **increasing significantly** for several years.*

13) Further research is being conducted to study MRSA.

The correct answer is TRUE because the passage states *Scientific trials are testing whether MRSA develops resistance after exposure to new drugs. A research breakthrough would herald a cure for the MRSA threat.*

14) Penicillin is an effective treatment for MRSA.

The correct answer is FALSE because the passage refers to MRSA having *developed a resistance to penicillin.*

15) MRSA can prove fatal.

The correct answer is TRUE because the passage refers to MRSA as a cause of death.

There are now several million cars in the UK using satellite navigation systems (satnav systems). These increasingly popular satnav systems mean that motorists no longer have to read maps while they are driving. There are two other major advantages: reduced journey time and reduced mileage (and thus fuel consumption) on unfamiliar routes. System improvements have made these devices much more accurate than earlier models, and today's designs are easier to use and have fewer distracting features. Although some safety surveys highlight the dangers of operating dashboard devices while driving, research conducted by one satnav manufacturer showed that nearly 70 per cent of drivers felt calmer and more focused on the road when using a satnav system.

16) Most drivers feel calmer when using a satnav system.

The correct answer is TRUE because the passage states: *other research shows that nearly 70 per cent of drivers felt calmer and more focused on the road when using a satnav system.*

17) Controversy remains about the effects that satnav systems have on driver concentration.

The correct answer is TRUE because the passage states

that: *Although some safety surveys highlight the dangers of operating dashboard devices while driving, other research shows that
nearly 70 per cent of drivers felt calmer and more focused on the
road when using a satnav system.*

18) Satellite navigation systems are useful for those people who
can't read maps.
The correct answer is TRUE based on the following extract:
motorists no longer have to read maps while they are driving.

19) The passage suggests that a satnav system can make navigation more efficient.
The correct answer is TRUE because the passage states:
*There are two other major advantages: reduced journey time and
reduced mileage (and thus fuel consumption) on unfamiliar
routes.*

20) Early satnav systems were less accurate than modern ones.
The correct answer is TRUE because of the following
extract: *System improvements have made these devices much
more accurate than earlier models.*

*Peru's Machu Picchu has been a popular tourist destination since it
was discovered in 1911. These mountain-top ruins have become one of
the most famous symbols of the Incan empire. The difficult terrain surrounding Machu Picchu meant that Spanish conquistadors never
discovered the city. It has been theorised, given the virtual inaccessibility of the site, that it was built for religious – rather than economic
or military – reasons. This UNESCO world heritage site's 200 buildings include many temples and houses. The construction of these
buildings relied upon cutting many perfectly fitting granite blocks
without the use of mortar.*

21) Machu Picchu served as a religious centre.
The correct answer is CAN'T TELL because the passage
states *it has been theorised, given the virtual inaccessibility of the
site, that it was built for religious – rather than economic or*

military – reasons. In other words there are different theories – none of which have been proved – about the purpose of Machu Picchu.

22) Machu Picchu is a ruined city in Peru.
The correct answer is TRUE because the first two lines in the passage mention *Peru's Machu Picchu* and *mountain-top ruins.*

23) Machu Picchu was built in 1911.
The correct answer is FALSE because the passage states that it was *discovered in 1911.*

24) Its valley location protected Machu Picchu from the Spanish conquistadors.
The correct answer is FALSE because the second and third lines of the passage mention *mountain-top ruins* and *difficult terrain.* Thus while it was the terrain that protected Machu Picchu it was not located in a valley.

25) Skilled stonemasons were involved in Machu Picchu's construction.
The correct answer is TRUE because the passage mentions that the *buildings were constructed using perfectly fitting granite blocks without the use of mortar.*

Over the last ten years the reach and the sophistication of international supply chains has increased. The three main factors influencing global supply chain design are manufacturing operations, distribution and transportation. These logistic networks connect the supplier's base to its end customer goods and services. There are always several companies seeking to maximise their own profits in any single global supply chain. But it is in the interest of each company in the chain to deal with the others fairly, as their mutual success depends on every link in the chain operating efficiently. Failure can also be shared. A supplier experiencing financial difficulties can soon pass its credit problems to other companies – even to more profitable

organisations – along the lines of their interconnected supply chain.
There are practical measures for avoiding such contagion from
defaulting suppliers or manufacturers. One such safety net involves
building a network of multiple suppliers, multiple production facilities
and multiple storage facilities – though this, of course, is not always
possible for smaller companies.

26) Every company in a supply chain should try to make the maximum profit.

    The correct answer is FALSE. While the passage says that *There are always several companies seeking to maximise their own profits in any single global supply chain*, the next sentence says that fair dealing between supply chain companies is essential to success.

27) Manufacturing companies who default can spread their credit problems throughout the supply system.

    The correct answer is TRUE because the passage describes how: *A supplier experiencing financial difficulties can soon pass its credit problems to other companies – even to more profitable organisations – along the lines of their interconnected supply chain.*

28) International supply chains are planned around only three considerations.

    The correct answer is FALSE because the passage describes: *The three* main *factors influencing global supply chain design are manufacturing operations, distribution and transportation.* Thus the passage suggests that there are more minor considerations.

29) The most sophisticated supply chains have a global reach.

    The correct answer is CAN'T TELL. The passage does say: *Over the last ten years the reach and the sophistication of international supply chains has increased.* However there is insufficient information to conclude that the most sophisticated supply chains are those with a global reach.

30) There is an indiscriminate impact throughout a supply chain if a supplier is experiencing credit difficulties.

The correct answer is TRUE because the passage explains that credit problems can be passed to *other companies – even to more profitable companies – along the lines of their interconnected supply chain,* i.e. the impact does not discriminate.

Digital broadcasting heralds a new paradigm in television broadcasting. This sophisticated broadcasting technology allows broadcasters to offer television with multiple broadcasting choices and interactive capabilities and high-quality sound and image. However, digital broadcasting should not be confused with High-Definition Television, which offers the very best audio and picture clarity. Analogue television may soon become obsolete in the UK. The USA has already made the transition from analogue to digital broadcasting. There, television stations have stopped broadcasting along analogue channels, and any viewers with analogue television sets must use special set-top conversion boxes in order to view programmes. As well as benefiting viewers with superior entertainment options, the switch to digital broadcasting frees up part of the valuable broadcasting spectrum that can then be used for public and emergency services.

31) Digital television offers the best audio and visual quality.

The correct answer is FALSE. The passage states: *High-Definition Television, which offers the very best audio and picture clarity.*

32) In the USA, analogue televisions can no longer be used.

The correct answer is FALSE. The passage explains that analogue televisions can still be used with set-top conversion boxes.

33) The switch to digital broadcasting benefits the emergency services.

The correct answer is TRUE. The passage states that: *the switch to digital broadcasting frees up part of the valuable broad-*

casting spectrum that can then be used for pubic and emergency services.

34) The UK will soon convert from analogue to digital broadcasting.

The correct answer is CAN'T TELL. The passage says *Analogue television may soon become obsolete in the UK* but there is no mention of definitive conversion plans.

35) A set-top box is necessary in order to access digital broadcasts.

The correct answer is FALSE. A set-top box is only necessary for viewers with analogue televisions.

Wildlife expert Dr Boyle spoke at this year's Wildlife Conservation Conference about the lack of a strategy to prevent the imminent extinction of a number of primate species across Asia. Her talk focused on the dangers of hunters and the clearing of tropical rainforests across the continent. Several species of Asian monkeys, some only recently discovered, are facing these dual threats to their natural habitats. Dr Boyle differentiated the most at-risk primates as critically endangered, but the talk stressed that other species were also living under constant threat. Dr Boyle's scientific paper presented compelling evidence of the need to halt deforestation, but in some developing Asian economies, where wood is collected for fuel and for sale and land is cleared for farming, human interests currently take precedence over the fate of the region's lower-order primates.

36) One of the attendees of this year's Wildlife Conservation Conference was called Dr Boyle.

The correct answer is TRUE because the passage describes Dr Boyle speaking at this year's Wildlife Conservation Conference.

37) The passage gives three reasons for the destruction of tropical rainforests.

The correct answer is TRUE because the passage describes

the following three reasons; collecting wood for fuel and for sale and clearing the land for farming.

38) All Asian primates are threatened by extinction.

The correct answer is FALSE. The first sentence in the passage refers to the *imminent extinction of a number of primate species across Asia* and later in the passage it refers to *several species of Asian monkeys, some only recently discovered.* This does not mean *all* Asian primates.

39) Asian monkeys are the most at risk.

The correct answer is CAN'T TELL because the passage states that *Dr Boyle differentiated the most at-risk primates as critically endangered, but the talk stressed that other species were also living under constant threat.* However there is no information on which animals are the most at risk.

40) Several types of Asian monkey live in the tropical rainforests.

The correct answer is TRUE. The relevant parts of the passage are as follows: *the clearing of tropical rainforests across the continent; and **Several species of Asian monkey**, some only recently discovered, are facing these dual threats to their natural habitats.*

Critics of modern quasi-non-governmental organisations point to their remoteness, lack of accountability and the difficulty of managing such bureaucratic organisations. Quangos, which operate at arm's length from the government, are often viewed by the public as inefficient and ineffective, spending more time talking about their goals than actually achieving them. Controversial though they may be, there is evidence of a rise in the number of quangos in the UK, though many of these state-run organisations use alternative names such as executive agency, board, council or commission. A recent report that the UK's quangos spent over £1 billion last year on public relations and communications is not likely to improve these organisations' popularity with taxpayers.

41) Modern quangos are entirely independent of government.

The correct answer is FALSE because the passage refers to: *Quangos, which operate at arm's length from the government* ... The question hinges on what is meant by operating at arm's length, which is that while there is some independent control it is not completely independent control.

42) 'Quango' is another way of referring to a quasi-non-governmental organisation.

The correct answer is TRUE because the passage starts by talking about *modern quasi-non-governmental organisations* and then at the start of the second sentence refers again to these entities as *quangos*.

43) The public perceive quangos as inefficient because of their marketing spend.

The correct answer is FALSE because the passage suggests that the public already perceives quangos as inefficient, whereas the report about spending on PR and communications is recent.

44) The passage suggests that quangos are bureaucratic.

The correct answer is TRUE because the passage states *Critics of modern quasi-non-governmental organisations point to their remoteness, lack of accountability and the difficulty of managing such bureaucratic organisations.*

45) The terms 'executive agency' and 'quango' are interchangeable.

The correct answer is TRUE because the passage refers to: *evidence of a rise in the number of quangos in the UK, though many of these state-run organisations use alternative names such as executive agency, board, council or commission.*

Last month the market research company Du Balle Inc. reported that the organic food sector grew over the past year, but not at the same rate as the previous five years in which the market grew fivefold. An oft-asked question about organic food is – why does it cost so much more? The simple answer is that organically grown products cost more to farm than their conventionally produced counterparts. Higher production costs due to methods such as crop rotation, hand-weeding (rather than pesticides) and the use of animal manure (instead of chemical fertilizers) result in higher costs to the consumer. Sceptics claim that organic foods are no healthier than non-organic foods. But proponents of organic farming counter that organically produced foods contain fewer contaminants – and that these health benefits more than justify the price differential. A spokeswoman from the Organic Farming Association said, 'Organic farming is about sustainability – and this means economic sustainability for struggling farmers, as well as sustainable food production.'

46) Growth in the organic food market is slowing.

The correct answer is TRUE according to the passage's first sentence. *Last month the market research company Du Balle Inc. reported that the organic food sector grew over the past year, but not at the same rate as for the previous five years in which the market grew fivefold.*

47) Using animal manure costs more than chemical fertilizers.

The correct answer is TRUE, because the passage explains that using organic farming methods, such as animal manure, costs more than conventional ones: *Higher production costs due to methods such as crop rotation, hand-weeding (rather than pesticides) and animal manure (instead of chemical fertilizers . . .*

48) Organically grown food is healthier.

The correct answer is CAN'T TELL. The passage suggests that there is controversy over the health benefits of organic food: *Sceptics claim that organic foods are no healthier than non-organic foods. But proponents of organic farming counter that organically produced foods contain fewer contaminants . . .*

49) Organically grown food contains no pesticides and contaminants.

The correct answer is FALSE. The passage states that:
organically produced foods contain fewer contaminants. Fewer
suggests that there are still some contaminants.

50) Organic farms are profitable.

The correct answer is CAN'T TELL. The passage refers to
organic farming as a growing market, but the quote from
the Organic Farming Association refers to *economic sustainability for struggling farmers.* It is impossible to say whether
organic farms are profitable.

*The Arctic region around the North Pole lacks specific land bound-
aries and has alternative definitions, such as its distinctive ecology.
The Arctic region's ecosystem is comprised of many species of plant,
bird, fish and mammal, including polar bears. There is life above,
below and even within this huge ocean of ice. But the natural habitat
of these Arctic animals is being threatened by the effects of global
warming. Typically the North Pole's ice cap diminishes in summer and
then replenishes itself in winter months. However, scientists speculate
that warmer oceans are causing a dramatic thinning of the Arctic's ice
during winter that has resulted in ice-free gaps of ocean in the summer.
Some experts predict that the entire ice cap will have disappeared by
the end of this century.*

51) Marine mammals are the only things living in the Arctic.

The correct answer is FALSE because the passage states
that *The Arctic region's ecosystem is comprised of many species
of plant, bird, fish and mammal, including polar bears.*

52) The Arctic's seasonal pattern is to reduce in size during the
winter months.

The correct answer is FALSE because the passage states
that the Arctic *replenishes itself in winter months.*

53) Higher seawater temperatures are making the Arctic melt.

The correct answer is CAN'T TELL because the passage states that *scientists speculate that warmer oceans are causing a dramatic thinning of the Arctic's ice . . .*

54) The Arctic has fixed geographic borders.

The correct answer is FALSE because the passage says *The Arctic region around the North Pole lacks specific land boundaries . . .*

55) All of the Arctic's ice disappears in the summer.

The correct answer is FALSE. The passage mentions gaps in the ice during summer: *ice-free gaps of ocean in the summer.*

Ethical labels are now widely used on products, such as coffee, to show that the goods in question have been produced in a worker-friendly manner. A ban on child workers is one labour practice to which ethically labelled suppliers must strictly adhere. Despite increased public awareness, many UK retail stories may still be selling products produced by foreign workers paid extremely low wages. Although working conditions have improved in some companies as a result of labelling, sweatshop wages and a lack of union representation remain prevalent in other suppliers from developing countries. There is also a danger that, where ethical codes of practice have been implemented, the supply workers themselves are inadvertently punished with lower pay.

56) Developing countries restrict union representation.

The correct answer is CAN'T TELL. The passage notes *. . . a lack of union representation remain[s] prevalent in other suppliers from developing countries.* However it would be wrong to say definitively that developing countries restricted union representation.

57) The use of ethical labelling has not improved working conditions.

The correct answer is FALSE. The passage states that *working conditions have improved in some companies as a result of labelling . . .*

58) Ethical labelling as an industry is in decline.

The correct answer is FALSE because the passage states that *Ethical labels are now widely used.*

59) The implementation of ethical codes of practice never back-fires on workers.

The correct answer is FALSE. The passage refers to the *danger that, where ethical codes of practice have been implemented, the supply workers themselves are inadvertently punished with lower pay.*

60) The passage suggests that using ethical labels on products can have both a beneficial and a detrimental effect.

The correct answer is TRUE since the passage refers to an improvement: *Although working conditions have improved in some companies as a result of labelling . . .* but also states: *There is also a danger that, where ethical codes of practice have been implemented, the supply workers themselves are inadvertently punished with lower pay.*

The UK has a target of cutting its carbon emissions by using renewable sources to generate a third of its electricity by 2020. One option is to invest heavily in building thousands of wind farms around the country. But a key technological issue that remains to be solved is how to efficiently store wind-powered electricity so as to ensure the regularity of supply that is needed by consumers. Other solutions for cutting carbon emissions are to increase the amount of the electricity supplied by nuclear power or to build more coal-fired power stations equipped with carbon capture technology. The carbon capture technology reduces greenhouse gas emissions by capturing and storing carbon dioxide.

61) Wind-powered electricity needs to be stored before being distributed to consumers.

The correct answer is TRUE because the passage explains, when discussing wind energy, that there is a need *to efficiently store wind-powered electricity so as to ensure the regularity of supply that is needed by consumers.*

62) The passage suggests that carbon capture technology reduces carbon dioxide emissions from coal-fired power stations.

The correct answer is TRUE. The relevant part of the passage is as follows: *Other solutions are to . . . build more coal-fired power stations equipped with carbon capture technology. The carbon capture technology reduces greenhouse gas emissions by capturing and storing carbon dioxide.* In other words, the technology stores carbon dioxide rather than releasing it as emissions.

63) The UK is on track to meet its 2020 target.

The correct answer is CAN'T TELL since the passage does not describe the UK's progress towards the target.

64) Wind farms are a renewable source of energy.

The correct answer is TRUE since the second sentence refers to wind farming as an option for reaching the renewable energy target.

65) The passage considers nuclear power to be a renewable source of energy.

The correct answer is TRUE based on the following extracts: *The UK has a target of cutting its carbon emissions by using renewable sources to generate a third of its electricity by 2020* and then later in the passage *Other solutions for cutting carbon emissions are to increase the amount of the electricity supplied by nuclear power . . .*

There are several thousand patients waiting for organ transplants in the UK. This urgent need has led to a government review of how best to increase organ donation rates. The introduction of presumed consent – as found in other European countries – has now been put forward as a possible solution. Such a drastic and controversial change, whereby donating organs would become the default option, would require a new legal framework. Among many other proposals, the government's review recommended establishing the following: locally adapted national policies for organ donation; a best practice framework; and a national organisation to coordinate transplants.

66) Presumed consent means that donating your bodily organs is the default option.

The correct answer is TRUE. The passage explains that a switch to presumed consent would be a drastic change. Currently, the default option is to *not* donate your organs. But under presumed consent *donating organs would become the default option.*

67) More coordinators are being recruited to organise organ transplants.

The correct answer is CAN'T TELL because the passage refers to *many other proposals* without giving details of these other proposals. While it is highly likely that more coordinators will be needed there is insufficient information in the passage to state this definitively. It is also uncertain whether particular proposals are being implemented.

68) The number of patients waiting for transplants led to the government's review of the current situation.

The correct answer is TRUE because the passage states: *There are several thousand patients waiting for organ transplants in the UK. This urgent need has led to a government review . . .*

69) One recommendation was to introduce a standard national policy for all hospitals.

The correct answer is FALSE. The relevant part of the passage reads as follows: *the government's review recommended establishing the following:* **locally adapted national** *policies for organ donation . . .* While a new national policy for organ donation has been recommended, the passage provides further stipulation that the policies are to be adapted for local use.

70) Although it had widespread support, presumed consent was not part of the government's recommendations.

The correct answer is FALSE. Although it is true that the government did not recommend a policy of presumed consent, the passage refers to the introduction of presumed consent as a *controversial change* so it is false to say it had widespread support.

CHAPTER 10

Graduate and managerial level verbal reasoning tests

You may be wondering why you need to take a verbal reasoning test if you have already studied for a degree or proven yourself in a business environment. However, in today's fiercely competitive business world, organisations only want to appoint the most promising candidates. As the number of graduates has risen, employers have turned to ability tests, such as verbal reasoning tests, to distinguish between large numbers of highly qualified applicants. Finding the right person for a job is always important, and it is never more so than at the senior management level when an inappropriate selection can be a costly and time-consuming mistake. That's why organisations use objective tests to assess candidates' high-level verbal reasoning skills and sift out unsuitable applicants for top jobs.

What does it test?

As with the previous chapter's UKCAT questions, graduate and managerial level verbal reasoning tests often have a passage-based format, whereby you read a passage of text and answer related questions. However these more advanced passages are often set in a financial or business context. This format is used across a range of graduate and managerial positions, though the content and level of difficulty of the questions vary. Just as managers have to make business decisions based on the information available, these tests require you to think logically about the information given to you in the passage.

Who takes it?

This popular test format is frequently used as part of the recruitment process. If you are a graduate on the milk round, you are very likely to encounter this sort of test. They are an effective and efficient way to assess a large number of candidates' verbal reasoning skills. You may also encounter this format of verbal reasoning test when applying for a first job, a new job or a promotion. For senior managerial roles, however, the verbal information that you will be analysing is likely to be more complex.

These tests are also used in other contexts. You could be tested as part of a development programme or if you are receiving career guidance. For example, managers of a development centre may be tested to see how they fare when asked to interpret more complex verbal information. This makes sense when you think about the verbal reasoning skills that managers need to develop when presenting complex information, either orally or in a written report.

Additional resources

There are many websites that offer free practice opportunities for this popular test format. Do an internet search of 'verbal reasoning test practice' and take your pick of the sites! University careers websites are a rich source of further practice and guidance on graduate recruitment processes. For example, City University's Careers Service has an up-to-date list of practice websites that are free at:

http://delicious.com/city_careers/PsychometricTests

The University of Bournemouth Graduate Employment Service also provides a comprehensive list of websites that offer practice tests:

www.bournemouth.ac.uk/careers/interviews

Sites such as these also contain downloadable information sheets on other parts of the graduate recruitment process, such as telephone interviewing, face-to-face interviewing and attending an assessment centre.

Instructions

Read the passage. To each question, answer TRUE, FALSE or CAN'T TELL using only the information given in the passage. Answer TRUE if the statement is true or follows on logically from the passage. Answer FALSE if the statement is false. Answer CAN'T TELL if there is insufficient information given in the passage.

Most graduate level verbal reasoning tests have around 40–55 questions. Depending upon the test's level of difficulty you will have between 20 and 35 minutes to answer the questions.

brilliant tip

While many graduate level verbal reasoning tests have the TRUE/FALSE/CAN'T TELL format, some tests will ask different types of questions about the passage. For example, you may be asked which sentence best summarises the passage, or which word could be substituted for another in the passage. If you want to practise these types of question, see the reading comprehension section in Chapter 8 and the Navy Verbal Ability practice questions in Chapter 7.

How to approach the questions

When doing this sort of test you need to differentiate between shades of grey. Remember that your objectivity is being tested. Base your answers only on the information provided in the passage.

When you analyse a complex passage you can break it down by asking yourself a series of questions. Apply these questions to the passage as a whole as well as to individual sentences. It is worth going through this process so that you do not misinterpret the information.

- What is the passage saying? What is fact? What is implied? What is only opinion?

- Is this an assertion based on emotion or opinion? Or a reasoned argument where factual evidence has been given to support the statement?

- If the passage makes inferences and deductions, is the conclusion it reaches true? Test out the reasoning before assuming it to be true.

When tackling a question, first ask yourself if the statement is 100 per cent true. If yes, you know that answer option A is correct. If the answer is no then you need to ask yourself: is the question 100 per cent false? If it is, then you know that answer option B is correct. This sounds simple enough. Many people struggle with the third multiple choice option – CAN'T TELL. If you are in any doubt about whether a question is entirely true or false then you need to consider answer option C as a possibility. Before you answer CAN'T TELL, double-check that you have a specific reason for not being able to tell.

See Chapter 4 for much more advice about how to approach passage-based tests.

brilliant tips

- Often the questions will get progressively harder. Use this bit of knowledge to your advantage: don't miss out questions early on. You need to build up a head of steam before reaching the more difficult questions!

- As the passages get more complex, you might find it worthwhile to attempt the shorter passages before the longer ones.

- When checking your answer, use your finger to underline the actual part of the passage that has led you to give that answer. If you can't point to it then you might want to rethink your answer!

Practice questions

For small to medium-sized businesses, outsourcing payroll operations is almost certainly a way to save time and staff costs. Payroll-service providers utilise specially designed computer systems, resulting in greater speed, accuracy and flexibility than an in-house department. Outsourcing the time-consuming burden of payroll administration enables businesses to be more focused and productive. However, organisations which outsource their payroll functions should remember that employers are ultimately accountable for the payment of their employees' income tax and national insurance payments – and should thus choose their provider wisely.

1) Large businesses would not benefit from outsourcing payroll operations.

   True/False/Can't tell

2) Fraudulent payroll-service providers can be held responsible for an employer's non-payment of taxes.

   True/False/Can't tell

3) One possible benefit of outsourcing payroll operations is reduced employee overheads.

   True/False/Can't tell

4) The passage states that small businesses can always save money by outsourcing payroll functions.

True/False/Can't tell

5) The passage suggests that payroll-service providers will make fewer mistakes than in-house payroll staff.

True/False/Can't tell

Conglomerate Plc, which supplies over 20,000 products to retailers in 50 countries and purchases parts from 312 factories, has one of the world's most sophisticated supply chains. This close collaboration with suppliers adds value to its business and reaps commercial advantage. At the same time Conglomerate Plc prides itself on considering the macroeconomic impact of social and environmental factors, in its dealings with supply chain partners. Although Conglomerate Plc's ultra-efficient supply chain benefits consumers by lowering retail prices, critics of this manufacturing giant purport that the constant pressure on its suppliers to cut costs has a negative impact on workers' pay and benefits.

6) Conglomerate Plc takes two macroeconomic factors into account when making supply chain decisions.

True/False/Can't tell

7) The passage suggests that global supply chains are of universal benefit.

True/False/Can't tell

8) Conglomerate Plc operates in more than 50 countries and has 312 factories.

True/False/Can't tell

9) Conglomerate Plc does not sell its products direct to the consumer.

True/False/Can't tell

10) Conglomerate Plc has unpredictable delivery systems.

True/False/Can't tell

According to recently published figures, internet sales last year comprised nearly 5 per cent of the UK's retail spending. It was the only retail channel showing growth, with a 20 per cent rise on the previous year's sales. The flourishing of e-commerce can be largely attributed to the increasing popularity of online super-market shopping and shoppers' preference for staying at home. The UK leads its European neighbours in internet shopping revenue, in part because of higher credit card usage than coun-tries such as Germany and France. Compared with continental Europe, the UK also has higher levels of computer ownership and wider access to the broadband services that facilitate internet purchases. Business experts forecast a trebling of internet retail sales in the UK and France over the next five years.

11) Sales trends for internet shopping in Germany have mir-rored those in the UK.

True/False/Can't tell

12) The UK is at the forefront of increasing European internet sales.

True/False/Can't tell

13) The passage suggests that internet shopping appeals to con-sumers who do not like going out to shop at shopping centres.

True/False/Can't tell

14) Low credit card usage is the only reason that continental European countries lag behind the UK in internet retail.

True/False/Can't tell

15) Internet retail sales in the UK and France will be higher next year.

True/False/Can't tell

The Board of Directors of Fone Industries (together with its subsidiaries) wishes to inform shareholders in the Company, as well as potential investors, that the consolidated net profit of the Group for the current quarter is expected to show a significant decline compared to that for the previous quarter. We attribute this unprecedented fall to the global economic downturn that has resulted in a drastic reduction in consumer spending on telecommunication products – and mobile handsets in particular. Fone Industries believes that our diverse product portfolio, respected brand and competitive pricing will enable us to weather the current economic situation. The information contained in this announcement is a preliminary assessment; full results for the year will be disclosed in the annual report to be published in April.

16) The global economy has been in recession for the past two quarters.

True/False/Can't tell

17) Fone Industries has suffered a nosedive in profits and is now operating at a loss.

True/False/Can't tell

18) Fone Industries' profits for the current quarter are predicted to be lower than those of the previous quarter.

True/False/Can't tell

19) Fone Industries is paying the price for the poor quality of its mobile phone handsets.

True/False/Can't tell

A worldwide economic recession has negatively impacted retail sales of telephones.

True/False/Can't tell

According to the Business School Admission Council, last year applications for full-time MBA programmes declined at 75 per cent of educational institutions offering the degree, with applications down by more than 20 per cent at over half of the schools surveyed. MBAs have traditionally been seen as a fast track to higher salaries and senior management positions, but the proliferation of MBA programmes has raised questions about the value of the degree. Business schools argue that they offer essential management training, and point to a poll of recent MBA graduates, over 80 per cent of whom rated their programmes as 'excellent'. But critics remain unconvinced that the MBA remains a necessary qualification for a high power career. Chris Wilson, Senior Partner at Wilson Recruitment & Selection, says, 'An MBA, even from a top-tier school, is no substitute for experience and a successful performance record.' Given the expense of full-time programmes, it is perhaps unsurprising that application figures for part-time executive MBA programmes increased by 50 per cent last year.

21) Some sceptics suggest that the MBA degree has been undermined by the plethora of programmes on offer.

   True/False/Can't tell

22) Last year part-time MBA programmes received more applications than traditional full-time courses.

   True/False/Can't tell

23) The quality of MBA courses has declined as the number of programmes on offer has increased.

   True/False/Can't tell

24) The passage argues that there is no longer any value in attaining an MBA.

True/False/Can't tell

25) The passage suggests that MBAs have historically been a prerequisite for an accelerated career.

True/False/Can't tell

The average British company uses only 55 per cent of its office space and two-thirds of employees are unhappy with their work environment, according to a survey recently undertaken by the design consultancy Best Desks Consultancy. This inefficient use of space equates to over £10 billion of waste in London alone. The advent of wireless technology means that employees need no longer be tied to fixed workstations with wires and cables and can work more flexibly. Trend forecasters predict the following innovations to workspaces over the next decade: more collaborative open-plan spaces to encourage social networking; reservable mobile workstations; easily interlockable office furniture; and bespoke ambient sound and lighting.

26) Staff productivity would be improved if workspaces were more appealingly designed.

True/False/Can't tell

27) The passage suggests that most British companies should move into smaller premises, thus saving money.

True/False/Can't tell

28) Current working environments could be more personalised to suit how individual employees like to work.

True/False/Can't tell

29) Two-thirds of British workers are dissatisfied with their jobs.

True/False/Can't tell

30) Flexible working has been facilitated by the rise of wireless technology.

True/False/Can't tell

At a time of tumbling share prices and longer life expectancy, many companies have acute shortfalls in their pension funds. Pension schemes in the UK are protected by a government fund contributed to by companies themselves, but British business has been lobbying for a change of rules in instances of company restructuring. A company is currently required to fully cover its pension liabilities when disposing of a division – a rule seen by some as obstructive to corporate activity. In theory, new legislation could allow businesses to transfer their pension liabilities to other divisions. However critics believe that this could give organisations carte blanche to shift their pension obligations to entities likely to become insolvent, thus forcing other organisations to subsidise their pension commitments.

31) British business believes that existing pension legislation impedes restructuring.

True/False/Can't tell

32) The passage cites three main reasons for deficits in companies' pension funds.

True/False/Can't tell

33) Current legislation allows British businesses to default on their pension obligations when they restructure.

True/False/Can't tell

34) Controversy surrounds any relaxation of pension rules associated with restructuring.

True/False/Can't tell

35) A change in pension legislation will help companies to reduce the hole in their pension schemes.

True/False/Can't tell

Pill-Tech Pharmaceutical today announced its definitive agreement to purchase Sosa Labs, a privately owned biotechnology company, for $195 million. Hans Bitter, CEO of Pill-Tech, stated, 'Sosa Labs has the expertise – and now the resources – to develop new drugs for Pill-Tech based on genomics.' This is the third small biotech firm acquired by the pharmaceutical giant in as many months, an aggressive initiative fuelled by the impending patent expiration of four of Pill-Tech's best-selling drugs. One such medication, the antidepressant Dorvax, is responsible for a quarter of Pill-Tech's sales. Given the lengthy time frame and heavy expense of developing and marketing novel drugs, some industry analysts believe Pill-Tech should seek a merger partner with which to combine portfolios and cut operating costs. Despite questions over the company's ongoing acquisition strategy, its finances are solid with a market capitalisation of approximately $60 billion.

36) Pill-Tech's sales revenue will fall by a quarter as a consequence of the antidepressant Dorvax's patent expiry.

True/False/Can't tell

37) An alternative strategy for Pill-Tech's future would be to form an alliance with another large pharmaceutical company.

True/False/Can't tell

38) Uncertainty over Pill-Tech's future direction has had a negative impact on its economic position.

True/False/Can't tell

39) Newly developed drugs will offset the lost sales when generic versions of their best-selling medicines become available.

True/False/Can't tell

40) The passage suggests that it is likely that Pill-Tech will acquire more biotechnology companies.

True/False/Can't tell

An unprecedented escalation in oil prices is threatening the hegemony of long-distance global supply chains. The cost of shipping goods from overseas has risen by 40 per cent, thus eroding the competitive advantage of lower Asian wage costs. Companies that ship bulky, low-added-value goods are seeking alternative logistical solutions to reduce transport costs. One major manufacturer of paper products saved 500,000 gallons of fuel per year by relocating its distribution centres to facilitate shipping by rail. A switch to transporting wine by barge has enabled one supermarket chain to reduce its fleet of trucks by 5 per cent. Traditionally, American timber was shipped to China where it was made into furniture and then shipped back to the USA. But in the wake of rising energy costs, moribund domestic furniture-making centres are experiencing a resurgence. Likewise, the American steel industry has seen production rise by 12 per cent while China's steel exports are down by a quarter.

41) Companies that ship lightweight, high-value products from overseas are immune to rising oil costs.

True/False/Can't tell

42) In certain industries a shift to domestic production is occurring.

True/False/Can't tell

43) The American steel industry has benefited from rising oil prices.

True/False/Can't tell

44) American-produced steel is now cheaper than steel manufactured in China.

True/False/Can't tell

45) Given the current economic climate goods are no longer being produced in Asia for export overseas.

True/False/Can't tell

An organisation's human capital is an intangible asset and as such is difficult to quantify. However, the average cost of voluntary defection can be conservatively estimated at £50,000 per employee, including the expense of recruitment and training. As a reduction in staff turnover equates to cost savings, HR practitioners in every industry are implementing retention programmes into their human capital management frameworks. Remuneration is no longer the simple solution to retaining valuable employees. In a recent survey of professionals, over 35 per cent of the respondents rated work/life balance as their primary career concern. One way for organisations to measure employee satisfaction is by using attitudinal metrics, the data from which can be used to enact strategic change. The introduction of employee stock options is another way to increase a workforce's commitment and loyalty. When resources are limited, companies can design bespoke retention programmes for their highest-performing employees.

46) The value of an organisation's human capital can be quantified using data from employee surveys.

True/False/Can't tell

47) The passage suggests that financial compensation has been the primary way for organisations to retain high performers.

True/False/Can't tell

48) The cost of implementing a corporate retention scheme can be offset by saving on staff turnover.

True/False/Can't tell

49) Strategic change programmes are always based upon employee satisfaction survey results.

True/False/Can't tell

50) The passage suggests that company stock option schemes engender feelings of belonging among participants.

True/False/Can't tell

51) The passage suggests that there are manifold approaches to human capital retention.

True/False/Can't tell

Project management, the system of organising resources to achieve a finite long-term goal, contrasts starkly with process-based operations, such as traditional banking. When such process-based industries, which can be characterised by a functional execution of immediate tasks, embark on a project a clash of cultures almost inevitably ensues. But as the corporate world shifts towards an increasingly project-based model, managers within process-based businesses must be educated in project management. This does not simply mean training courses in the use of planning software, but rather the adoption of a completely different management methodology. Traditional hierarchies represent one challenge to project-based working, whereby the project's hierarchy supersedes organisational seniority. Another obstacle in reactive, process-based cultures is a resistance to planning, and a mindset that IT is peripheral, rather than integral, to business projects. These hurdles are indisputably worth overcoming, however, as acquiring project management capabilities enables businesses to function effectively in project mode while continuing to conduct their day-to-day operations efficiently.

52) When working on a project, senior staff might be accountable to a more junior project manager.

True/False/Can't tell

53) The passage indicates that project management methodologies are at odds with those of some industries.

True/False/Can't tell

54) Long-range planning is antithetical to the discipline of project management.

True/False/Can't tell

55) Training courses in planning software are sufficient for acquiring project management expertise.

True/False/Can't tell

IT has been used commercially for over 50 years, yet no standard terminology or system for measuring the value of IT expenditure exists. This lack of methodology can be explained by IT's intangible nature and a prevailing belief that IT is a necessary, and uncontrollable, expense. Ultimately any metric for assessing IT investment must determine whether it has increased income or decreased expenditure. It is far too simplistic to merely consider personnel cost savings resultant from IT investment. Similarly, to crudely define IT expenditure as only hardware, software and infrastructure would also be wrong – the time of managers and professionals must also be factored in. One of the main impediments to developing a process for analysing the cost/benefit of IT projects is a lack of ownership by senior management.

56) The passage outlines the predominant system for assessing the return on IT investment.

   True/False/Can't tell

57) An obstacle to measuring IT investment is a lack of management responsibility for such projects.

   True/False/Can't tell

58) The passage asserts that IT costs are intrinsically difficult to regulate.

   True/False/Can't tell

59) One way of measuring an IT development success is whether it increases income for the business.

   True/False/Can't tell

60) The cost of employing IT professionals sometimes exceeds any personnel costs savings resulting from an IT project.

   True/False/Can't tell

Answers

Question	Answer
1	CAN'T TELL
2	FALSE
3	TRUE
4	FALSE
5	TRUE
6	TRUE
7	FALSE

8	FALSE
9	CAN'T TELL
10	FALSE
11	FALSE
12	TRUE
13	TRUE
14	FALSE
15	CAN'T TELL
16	CAN'T TELL
17	FALSE
18	TRUE
19	FALSE
20	TRUE
21	TRUE
22	CAN'T TELL
23	CAN'T TELL
24	FALSE
25	TRUE
26	CAN'T TELL
27	FALSE
28	TRUE
29	FALSE
30	TRUE
31	TRUE
32	FALSE
33	FALSE
34	TRUE
35	CAN'T TELL
36	CAN'T TELL
37	TRUE
38	FALSE
39	CAN'T TELL
40	TRUE
41	CAN'T TELL
42	TRUE

43	TRUE
44	CAN'T TELL
45	FALSE
46	FALSE
47	TRUE
48	CAN'T TELL
49	FALSE
50	TRUE
51	TRUE
52	TRUE
53	TRUE
54	FALSE
55	FALSE
56	FALSE
57	TRUE
58	TRUE
59	TRUE
60	CAN'T TELL

Answer explanations

For small to medium-sized businesses, outsourcing payroll operations is almost certainly a way to save time and staff costs. Payroll-service providers utilise specially designed computer systems, resulting in greater speed, accuracy and flexibility than an in-house department. Outsourcing the time-consuming burden of payroll administration enables businesses to be more focused and productive. However, organisations that outsource their payroll functions should remember that employers are ultimately accountable for the payment of their employees' income tax and national insurance payments – and should thus choose their provider wisely.

1) Large businesses would not benefit from outsourcing payroll operations. (CAN'T TELL)

   The first sentence of the passage establishes that the piece is focusing on *small to medium-sized businesses*. While there is no mention of large businesses there is nothing in the passage to say that the benefits described could not also apply to large businesses. Hence the answer to the question is CAN'T TELL.

2) Fraudulent payroll-service providers can be held responsible for an employer's non-payment of taxes. (FALSE)
    The relevant part of the passage states that *organisations which outsource their payroll functions should remember that employers are ultimately accountable for the payment of their employees' income tax and national insurance payments.* In other words the employers – and not payroll-service providers – remain responsible. The answer is FALSE.

3) One possible benefit of outsourcing payroll operations is reduced employee overheads. (TRUE)
    In the words of the passage: *For small to medium-sized businesses, outsourcing payroll operations is almost certainly a way to save time and staff costs.* Thus often employee overheads (i.e. staff costs) can be reduced by outsourcing payroll operations. Thus this question's statement is TRUE.

4) The passage states that small businesses can always save money by outsourcing payroll functions. (FALSE)
    There are two key words that you need to focus on here. These are *almost certainly.* They appear in the first line, as follows: *For small to medium-sized businesses, outsourcing payroll operations is almost certainly a way to save time and staff costs.* Thus this question's statement is FALSE, since it stipulates that such businesses can ***always*** save money.

5) The passage suggests that payroll-service providers will make fewer mistakes than in-house payroll staff. (TRUE)
    One of the points made by the passage is of the improved accuracy (*. . . resulting in greater speed, accuracy and flexibility . . .*) that payroll-service providers can bring. Thus the answer to this question is TRUE.

Conglomerate Plc, which supplies over 20,000 products to retailers in 50 countries and purchases parts from 312 factories, has one of the world's most sophisticated supply chains. This close collaboration with suppliers adds value to its business and reaps commercial advantage. At the same time Conglomerate Plc prides itself on considering the macroeconomic impact of social and environmental factors, in its dealings with supply chain partners. Although Conglomerate Plc's ultra-efficient supply chain benefits consumers by lowering retail prices, critics of this manufacturing giant purport that the constant pressure on its suppliers to cut costs has a negative impact on workers' pay and benefits.

6)   Conglomerate Plc takes two macroeconomic factors into account when making supply chain decisions. (TRUE)
     The passage refers to two macroeconomic factors (social, environmental impacts) in the following sentence: *At the same time Conglomerate Plc prides itself on considering the macroeconomic impact of social and environmental factors, in its dealings with supply chain partners.* Hence the answer to this question is TRUE.

7)   The passage suggests that global supply chains are of universal benefit. (FALSE)
     The reason that this question is FALSE is the *negative impact on workers' pay and benefits* that the passage refers to.

8)   Conglomerate Plc operates in more than 50 countries and has 312 factories. (FALSE)
     The relevant part of the passage states that *Conglomerate Plc. . . supplies over 20,000 products to retailers in 50 countries and purchases parts from 312 factories.* This question highlights the importance of paying careful attention to each word in the question. In particular key words, such as *more than.* Conglomerate Plc only operates in 50 countries. No more. The answer is FALSE.

9) Conglomerate Plc does not sell its products direct to the consumer. (CAN'T TELL)

The answer to this question is CAN'T TELL since it definitely sells to retailers, but there is no way of telling whether or not Conglomerate Plc also sells direct to customers. You may think this is likely and so answer FALSE. However going only on the information in the passage, the answer has to be CAN'T TELL.

10) Conglomerate Plc has unpredictable delivery systems. (FALSE)

This question must be FALSE. The passage refers to the *ultra-efficiency* of the supply chain.

According to recently published figures, internet sales last year comprised nearly 5 per cent of the UK's retail spending. It was the only retail channel showing growth, with a 20 per cent rise on the previous year's sales. The flourishing of e-commerce can be largely attributed to the increasing popularity of online supermarket shopping and shoppers' preference for staying at home. The UK leads its European neighbours in internet shopping revenue, in part because of higher credit card usage than countries such as Germany and France. Compared with continental Europe, the UK also has higher levels of computer ownership and wider access to the broadband services that facilitate internet purchases. Business experts forecast a trebling of internet retail sales in the UK and France over the next five years.

11) Sales trends for internet shopping in Germany have mirrored those in the UK. (FALSE)

There are a couple of sentences in the passage that refer to Europe, although only one of these refers to Germany specifically: *The UK leads its European neighbours in internet shopping, in part because of higher credit card usage than countries such as Germany and France. Compared with continental Europe, the UK also has higher levels of computer ownership and wider access to the broadband services that facilitate internet purchases.* There is sufficient information to say that the UK is leading its European neighbours in the area of internet sales, including Germany. Thus the answer is FALSE.

12) The UK is at the forefront of increasing European internet sales. (TRUE)

   The key phrase in the passage is *The UK leads its European neighbours in internet shopping.* The key word here is *leads.* Thus it is TRUE that the UK is at the forefront of increasing European internet sales.

13) The passage suggests that internet shopping appeals to consumers who do not like going out to shop at shopping centres. (TRUE)

   The passage mentions shoppers' preference for staying at home and links this to the *flourishing of e-commerce.* Thus the statement is TRUE.

14) Low credit card usage is the only reason that continental European countries lag behind the UK in internet retail. (FALSE)

   This is a tricky question. Low credit card usage is indeed one of the reasons that the passage describes. However it is not the only reason and so the statement is FALSE. As the passage specifically states: *The UK leads its European neighbours in internet shopping,* **in part** *because of higher credit card usage.*

15) Internet retail sales in the UK and France will be higher next year. (CAN'T TELL)

   Another tricky question. The statement is making a prediction. When the passage refers to future internet retail sales it makes a different prediction: *Business experts forecast a trebling of internet retail sales in the UK and France over the next five years.* A forecast for the next five years does not necessarily mean that the growth will come next year. Although it could. Thus more information is required. The answer is CAN'T TELL.

The Board of Directors of Fone Industries (together with its subsidiaries) wishes to inform shareholders in the Company, as well as potential investors, that the consolidated net profit of the Group for the current quarter is expected to show a significant decline compared to that for the previous quarter. We attribute this unprecedented fall to the global economic downturn that has resulted in a drastic reduction in consumer spending on telecommunication products – and mobile handsets in particular. Fone Industries believes that our diverse product portfolio, respected brand and competitive pricing will enable us to weather the current economic situation. The information contained in this announcement is a preliminary assessment; full results for the year will be disclosed in the annual report to be published in April.

16) The global economy has been in recession for the past two quarters. (CAN'T TELL)

   The passage makes it clear that there is a *global economic downturn*. It does not refer to how long this *global economic downturn* has lasted. Fone Industries have experienced a downturn for one quarter. The answer has to be CAN'T TELL.

17) Fone Industries has suffered a nosedive in profits and is now operating at a loss. (FALSE)

   The passage refers to a slowdown in profits rather than operating at a loss. Hence the statement is FALSE.

18) Fone Industries' profits for the current quarter are predicted to be lower than those of the previous quarter. (TRUE)

   The passage states that *the consolidated net profit of the Group for the current quarter is expected to show a significant decline compared to that for the previous quarter.* So the answer is TRUE.

19) Fone Industries is paying the price for the poor quality of its mobile phone handsets. (FALSE)

The answer is FALSE since the passage describes only economic reasons for the fall in profits; *We attribute this unprecedented fall to the global economic downturn . . .* There is no mention of poor-quality products. In fact, Fone Industries' *respected brand* is mentioned.

20) A worldwide economic recession has impacted negatively on retail sales of telephones. (TRUE)

The relevant part of the passage is: *We attribute this unprecedented fall to the global economic downturn that has resulted in a drastic reduction in consumer spending on telecommunication products – and mobile handsets in particular.* So the answer is TRUE.

According to the Business School Admission Council, last year applications for full-time MBA programmes declined at 75 per cent of educational institutions offering the degree, with applications down by more than 20 per cent at over half of the schools surveyed. MBAs have traditionally been seen as a fast track to higher salaries and senior management positions, but the proliferation of MBA programmes has raised questions about the value of the degree. Business schools argue that they offer essential management training, and point to a poll of recent MBA graduates, over 80 per cent of whom rated their programmes as 'excellent'. But critics remain unconvinced that the MBA remains a necessary qualification for a high power career. Chris Wilson, Senior Partner at Wilson Recruitment & Selection, says, 'An MBA, even from a top-tier school, is no substitute for experience and a successful performance record.' Given the expense of full-time programmes, it is perhaps unsurprising that application figures for part-time executive MBA programmes increased by 50 per cent last year.

21) Some sceptics suggest that the MBA degree has been undermined by the plethora of programmes on offer. (TRUE)

The relevant part of the passage states that *the proliferation of MBA programmes has raised questions about the value of the degree*. Hence the statement is TRUE.

22) Last year part-time MBA programmes received more applications than traditional full-time courses. (CAN'T TELL)

The passage states that *last year applications for full-time MBA programmes declined at 75 per cent of educational institutions offering the degree, with applications down by more than 20 per cent at over half of the schools surveyed*. The number of applications for full-time MBAs has reduced. The passage also explains that *Given the expense of full-time programmes, it is perhaps unsurprising that application figures for part-time executive MBA programmes increased by 50 per cent last year*. However there is no mention of how part-time MBA programmes applications compare to full-time ones. So the answer is CAN'T TELL.

23) The quality of MBA courses has declined as the number of programmes on offer has increased. (CAN'T TELL)

You might think that this is TRUE or FALSE depending upon which part of the passage you focus on. In fact, there is contradictory evidence. Initially the passage says *the proliferation of MBA programmes has raised questions about the value of the degree*. Later it states: *a poll of recent MBA graduates, over 80 per cent of whom rated their programmes as 'excellent'*. The answer is that you CAN'T TELL.

24) The passage argues that there is no longer any value in attaining an MBA. (FALSE)

The passage provides a balanced perspective – rather than being for or against MBAs. Thus it would be FALSE to say that there is no longer any value in attaining an MBA.

25) The passage suggests that MBAs have historically been a prerequisite for an accelerated career. (TRUE)

The answer is TRUE because the passage explains that

MBAs have traditionally been seen as a fast track to higher salaries and senior management positions.

The average British company uses only 55 per cent of its office space and two-thirds of employees are unhappy with their work environment, according to a survey recently undertaken by the design consultancy Best Desks Consultancy. This inefficient use of space equates to over £10 billion of waste in London alone. The advent of wireless technology means that employees need no longer be tied to fixed workstations with wires and cables and can work more flexibly. Trend forecasters predict the following innovations to workspaces over the next decade: more collaborative open-plan spaces to encourage social networking; reservable mobile workstations; easily interlockable office furniture; and bespoke ambient sound and lighting.

26) Staff productivity would be improved if workspaces were more appealingly designed. (CAN'T TELL)

The passage presents arguments for designing work environments more efficiently. It also makes the point that employees *can work more flexibly*. But the passage does not explicitly state that productivity would be improved – this is conjecture so the answer is CAN'T TELL.

27) The passage suggests that most British companies should move into smaller premises, thus saving money. (FALSE)

Don't be misled into thinking that this statement is true by the sentence: *This inefficient use of space equates to over £10 billion of waste in London alone.* This is not a recommendation for companies to move to smaller premises. The answer is FALSE.

28) Current working environments could be more personalised to suit how individual employees like to work. (TRUE)

A prediction is made as follows: *Trend forecasters predict the following innovations to workspaces over the next decade: more collaborative open-plan spaces to encourage social networking; reservable mobile workstations; easily interlockable office furni-*

ture. The implication is that existing working environments could be tailored in the future. The statement is TRUE.

29) Two-thirds of British workers are dissatisfied with their jobs. (FALSE)

Survey evidence that *two-thirds of employees are unhappy with their work environment* is cited. But the passage does not state that they are unhappy with their jobs. Thus the answer is FALSE.

30) Flexible working has been facilitated by the rise of wireless technology. (TRUE)

The passage states *The advent of wireless technology means that employees need no longer be tied to fixed workstations with wires and cables and can work more flexibly.* Therefore the answer is TRUE.

At a time of tumbling share prices and longer life expectancy, many companies have acute shortfalls in their pension funds. Pension schemes in the UK are protected by a government fund contributed to by companies themselves, but British business has been lobbying for a change of rules in instances of company restructuring. A company is currently required to fully cover its pension liabilities when disposing of a division – a rule seen by some as obstructive to corporate activity. In theory, new legislation could allow businesses to transfer their pension liabilities to other divisions. However critics believe that this could give organisations carte blanche to shift their pension obligations to entities likely to become insolvent, thus forcing other organisations to subsidise their pension commitments.

31) British business believes that existing pension legislation impedes restructuring. (TRUE)

The answer is TRUE because the passage states that *British business has been lobbying for a change of rules in instances of company restructuring.*

32) The passage cites three main reasons for deficits in companies' pension funds. (FALSE)
Actually only two reasons are given. These are *tumbling share prices and longer life expectancy* . . . So the answer is FALSE.

33) Current legislation allows British businesses to default on their pension obligations when they restructure. (FALSE)
This is FALSE because the passage states that *A company is currently required to fully cover its pension liabilities when disposing of a division* . . .

34) Controversy surrounds the possibility of any relaxation of pension rules associated with restructuring. (TRUE)
The answer to this question is TRUE. This is because the passage argues both for and against the relaxation of pension rules about restructuring. Proponents believe that the current rule is: *obstructive to corporate activity. In theory, new legislation could allow businesses to transfer their pension liabilities to other divisions.* The passage goes on to give the argument against as follows: *However critics believe that this could give organisations carte blanche to shift their pension obligations to entities likely to become insolvent, thus forcing other organisations to subsidise their pension commitments.*

35) A change in pension legislation will help companies to reduce the hole in their pension schemes. (CAN'T TELL)
Although at the outset the passage clearly states that *many companies have acute shortfalls in their pension funds* the question of whether or not the proposed legislation will help companies to reduce the hole in their pension schemes is not discussed. Thus the answer to the question must be CAN'T TELL.

Pill-Tech Pharmaceutical today announced its definitive agreement to purchase Sosa Labs, a privately owned biotechnology company, for $195 million. Hans Bitter, CEO of Pill-Tech, stated, 'Sosa Labs has the expertise – and now the resources – to develop new drugs for Pill-Tech *based on genomics.' This is the third small biotech firm acquired by the pharmaceutical giant in as many months, an aggressive initiative fuelled by the impending patent expiration of four of Pill-Tech's best-selling drugs. One such medication, the antidepressant Dorvax, is responsible for a quarter of Pill-Tech's sales. Given the lengthy time frame and heavy expense of developing and marketing novel drugs, some industry analysts believe Pill-Tech should seek a merger partner with which to combine portfolios and cut operating costs. Despite questions over the company's ongoing acquisition strategy, its finances are solid with a market capitalisation of approximately $60 billion.*

36) Pill-Tech's sales revenue will fall by a quarter as a consequence of the antidepressant Dorvax's patent expiry. (CAN'T TELL)

   The passage says that *the antidepressant Dorvax, is responsible for a quarter of Pill-Tech's sales.* However, Dorvax's patent expiry does not necessarily mean that sales revenue will fall by a quarter. The answer has to be CAN'T TELL.

37) An alternative strategy for Pill-Tech's future would be to form an alliance with another large pharmaceutical company. (TRUE)

   This is TRUE, and is expressed as follows: *some industry analysts believe Pill-Tech should seek a merger partner with which to combine portfolios and cut operating costs.*

38) Uncertainty over Pill-Tech's future direction has had a negative impact on its economic position. (FALSE)

   The relevant part of the passage is: *Despite questions over the company's ongoing acquisition strategy, **its finances are solid** with a market capitalisation of approximately $60 billion.* The answer is FALSE – there has been no negative impact on Pill-Tech's finances.

39) Newly developed drugs will offset the lost sales when generic versions of their best-selling medicines become available. (CAN'T TELL)

This is tricky. The passage makes clear that Pill-Tech's strategy is to develop new drugs in order to compensate for lost sales as patents expire. However the question says *will* and there is no way of knowing for certain whether or not this strategy will be effective, so the answer has to be CAN'T TELL.

40) The passage suggests that it is likely that Pill-Tech will acquire more biotechnology companies. (TRUE)
Look carefully at the last line of the passage: *Despite questions over the company's ongoing acquisition strategy, its finances are solid with a market capitalisation of approximately $60 billion.* The word *ongoing* is a key. It means that the answer is TRUE .

An unprecedented escalation in oil prices is threatening the hegemony of long-distance global supply chains. The cost of shipping goods from overseas has risen by 40 per cent, thus eroding the competitive advantage of lower Asian wage costs. Companies that ship bulky, low-added-value goods are seeking alternative logistical solutions to reduce transport costs. One major manufacturer of paper products saved 500,000 gallons of fuel per year by relocating its distribution centres to facilitate shipping by rail. A switch to transporting wine by barge has enabled one supermarket chain to reduce its fleet of trucks by 5 per cent. Traditionally, American timber was shipped to China where it was made into furniture and then shipped back to the USA. But in the wake of rising energy costs, moribund domestic furniture-making centres are experiencing a resurgence. Likewise, the American steel industry has seen production rise by 12 per cent while China's steel exports are down by a quarter.

41) Companies that ship lightweight, high-value products from overseas are immune to rising oil costs. (CAN'T TELL)
The passage indicates that *Companies that ship bulky, low added-value goods are seeking alternative logistical solutions to reduce transport costs.* But this does not mean that their oppo-

site – lightweight, high-value items – are unaffected by rising oil costs. The answer is CAN'T TELL.

42) In certain industries a shift to domestic production is occurring. (TRUE)
The answer is TRUE. Two examples are given in the passage – the furniture-making and steel industries.

43) The American steel industry has benefited from rising oil prices. (TRUE)
The answer is TRUE. The passage states that *the American steel industry has seen production rise by 12 per cent.*

44) American-produced steel is now cheaper than steel manufactured in China. (CAN'T TELL)
Following on from the answer to question 43, we know that the American steel industry has benefited from rising oil prices. However we do not know the exact extent of this. It is not possible – based on the information in the passage – to say whether or not American-produced steel is now cheaper than steel manufactured in China. So the correct answer is CAN'T TELL.

45) Given the current economic climate goods are no longer being produced in Asia for export overseas. (FALSE)
The passage argues about the continuing economic viability for transporting goods long distance. For example from Asia: *The cost of shipping goods from overseas has risen by 40 per cent, thus eroding the competitive advantage of lower Asian wage costs.* Although some of the cost benefits have been eroded this does not mean that it is no longer financially viable to manufacture in Asia. There is no mention of goods no longer being produced in Asia for export overseas due to the economy, In fact the passage states that *China's steel exports are down by a quarter.* So China is still exporting. So the answer is FALSE.

An organisation's human capital is an intangible asset and as such is difficult to quantify. However, the average cost of voluntary defection can be conservatively estimated at £50,000 per employee, including the expense of recruitment and training. As a reduction in staff turnover equates to cost savings, HR practitioners in every industry are implementing retention programmes into their human capital management frameworks. Remuneration is no longer the simple solution to retaining valuable employees. In a recent survey of professionals, over 35 per cent of the respondents rated work/life balance as their primary career concern. One way for organisations to measure employee satisfaction is by using attitudinal metrics, the data from which can be used to enact strategic change. The introduction of employee stock options is another way to increase a workforce's commitment and loyalty. When resources are limited, companies can design bespoke retention programmes for their highest-performing employees.

46) The value of an organisation's human capital can be quantified using data from employee surveys. (FALSE)

The answer is FALSE based upon the opening statement that *An organisation's human capital is an intangible asset and as such is difficult to quantify.*

47) The passage suggests that financial compensation has been the primary way for organisations to retain high performers. (TRUE)

The answer is TRUE based upon the following statement: *Remuneration is no longer the simple solution to retaining valuable employees.*

48) The cost of implementing a corporate retention scheme can be offset by saving on staff turnover. (CAN'T TELL)

Do not be misled into thinking that this statement is TRUE. The passage states that *As a reduction in staff turnover equates to cost savings, HR practitioners in every industry are implementing retention programmes into their human capital management frameworks.* However, this does not mean that one equals or offsets the other. The answer is CAN'T TELL.

49) Strategic change programmes are always based upon employee satisfaction survey results. (FALSE)
The relevant part of the passage is as follows: *One way for organisations to measure employee satisfaction is by using attitudinal metrics, the data from which can be used to enact strategic change.* The answer is FALSE.

50) The passage suggests that company stock option schemes engender feelings of belonging among participants. (TRUE)
The answer is TRUE because of the statement: *The introduction of employee stock options is another way to increase a workforce's commitment and loyalty.*

51) The passage suggests that there are manifold approaches to human capital retention. (TRUE)
The passage describes many different ways of retaining employees, for example stock options, remuneration and satisfaction surveys. So the statement is TRUE.

Project management, the system of organising resources to achieve a finite long-term goal, contrasts starkly with process-based operations, such as traditional banking. When such process-based industries, which can be characterised by a functional execution of immediate tasks, embark on a project a clash of cultures almost inevitably ensues. But as the corporate world shifts towards an increasingly project-based model, managers within process-based businesses must be educated in project management. This does not simply mean training courses in the use of planning software, but rather the adoption of a completely different management methodology. Traditional hierarchies represent one challenge to project-based working, whereby the project's hierarchy supersedes organisational seniority. Another obstacle in reactive, process-based cultures is a resistance to planning, and a mindset that IT is peripheral, rather than integral, to business projects. These hurdles are indisputably worth overcoming, however, as acquiring project management capabilities enables businesses to function effectively in project mode while continuing to conduct their day-to-day operations efficiently.

52) When working on a project, senior staff might be accountable to a more junior project manager. (TRUE)
The following sentence is key: *Traditional hierarchies represent one challenge to project-based working, whereby the project's hierarchy supersedes organisational seniority.* The answer is TRUE.

53) The passage indicates that project management methodologies are at odds with those of some industries. (TRUE)
The answer is TRUE as the passage describes how project management *contrasts starkly with process-based operations, such as traditional banking.*

54) Long-range planning is antithetical to the discipline of project management. (FALSE)
The passage defines project management as *organising resources to achieve a finite long-term goal . . .* It is a system of long-range planning so the answer must be FALSE.

55) Training courses in planning software are sufficient for acquiring project management expertise. (FALSE)
The key words are *not simply* in the following sentence: *This does not simply mean training courses in the use of planning software, but rather the adoption of a completely different management methodology.* Software training courses are certainly an important part of acquiring project management skills, but they are not sufficient – they need to be accompanied by a change in methodology. So the answer is FALSE.

IT has been used commercially for over 50 years, yet no standard terminology or system for measuring the value of IT expenditure exists.

This lack of methodology can be explained by IT's intangible nature and a prevailing belief that IT is a necessary, and uncontrollable, expense. Ultimately any metric for assessing IT investment must determine whether it has increased income or decreased expenditure. It is far too simplistic to merely consider personnel cost savings resultant from IT investment. Similarly, to crudely define IT expenditure as only hardware, software and infrastructure would also be wrong – the time of managers and professionals must also be factored in. One of the main impediments to developing a process for analysing the cost/benefit of IT projects is a lack of ownership by senior management.

56) The passage outlines the predominant system for assessing the return on IT investment. (FALSE)

The opening sentence includes the phrase *no standard terminology or system for measuring the value of IT expenditure exists.* The rest of the passage does not outline a *dominant system for assessing the return on IT investment.* So the answer is FALSE.

57) An obstacle to measuring IT investment is a lack of management responsibility for such projects. (TRUE)

This is TRUE because the passage states that *One of the main impediments to developing a process for analysing the cost/benefit of IT projects is a lack of ownership by senior management.*

58) The passage asserts that IT costs are intrinsically difficult to regulate. (TRUE)

The passage states that: *This lack of methodology can be explained by IT's intangible nature and a prevailing belief that IT is a necessary, and uncontrollable, expense.* Thus the answer is TRUE.

59) One way of measuring an IT development's success is whether it increases income for the business. (TRUE)

This is TRUE, as the passage says: *Ultimately any metric for assessing IT investment must determine whether it has increased income or decreased expenditure.*

60) The cost of employing IT professionals sometimes exceeds any personnel cost savings resulting from an IT project. (CAN'T TELL)

The relevant part of the passage is: *Similarly, to crudely define IT expenditure as only hardware, software and infrastructure would also be wrong – the time of managers and professionals must also be factored in.* So both the cost of IT professionals and savings on personnel are certainly factors to be considered. However one CAN'T TELL whether one exceeds the other.

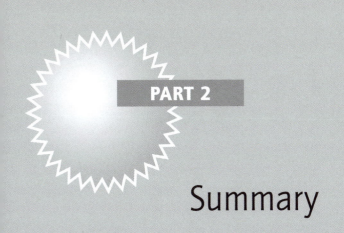

PART 2

Summary

f you've worked your way through the practice questions in Part 2 you should be feeling ready to tackle your verbal reasoning test. But first take a moment to give yourself a well-deserved high five. Way to go! You've done yourself a big favour by taking the time to prepare. All that practice for one test may seem like a lot of effort, but it is time well spent when your future is at stake. Whether you are hoping to get a place on a training course, your first job, or a challenging promotion, passing your verbal reasoning test will take you one step closer to your goal.

If you completed the practice questions relevant to your upcoming test – and maybe many other practice questions too – you should be feeling much more confident about your verbal reasoning skills. You'll also know what to expect on your test day, which will give you a valuable edge over the competition. Now you just need to stay calm and get a good night's sleep before the test. If you are worried about nerves getting the better of you on the big day, refer back to Chapter 3 for some advice on mental preparation.

If you are still worried that your verbal reasoning skills are not up to scratch, the best thing you can do is practise some more. Start with the easier chapters if you did not do this first time around. Pay close attention to the answer explanations so you are clear on where you are going wrong – and can avoid making the same mistakes again. Each chapter in Part 2 also includes an Additional Resources box. Use these to access additional practice questions and find out as much as you can about your test. Try not to get discouraged if you are not improving as much as you'd like. It takes time to hone new skills. If you practise enough, and learn from your mistakes, you will eventually see an improvement. The important thing is to keep a positive attitude.

It might not have been your intention when you picked up this book, but hopefully you have benefited from improving your verbal reasoning skills. If you've followed the suggestions in Chapter 5 and challenged yourself by reading more complex books, newspapers and magazines, you may want to continue reading at this higher level long after your test day has passed. Reading is, after all, a pleasure as well as a skill. And, if you continue to look up and learn new words, you are sure to impress friends and colleagues with your rich vocabulary.

I wish you a lot of luck on your test day. But if you apply all the strategies you've acquired through your practice sessions you don't need luck – you have all the tools you need for success. Just perform to the best of your ability and do yourself proud.